MORE THAN MEDICINE

BEING A CHRISTIAN PHYSICIAN IN A NON-CHRISTIAN WORLD

Michael Dodd, MD

1

The opinions and conclusions expressed in this study are those of the author. All references to websites, authors, publications, brand names and/or products are placed there by the author.

Cover Photography and Design by Robbie Gray and Clark Harrison

ISBN: 9781544261508

First Edition

CONTENTS

WEEK ONE

A CULTURE CHANGE, PART ONE

Day One

"Good morning! I'm Dr. Dodd. What brings you into the E.R. today?"

"Well, for the past couple of--wait, what was your name again?"

"Dr. Dodd."

"Oh, I thought you said Dr. God."

"No sir. I can assure you that there is only one Dr. God, and I'm not Him."

It's a conversation that I seem to have with a patient in the emergency department at least once a month, and unfortunately, I can't blame patients for being confused. I have met far too many physicians in America that act like they are God. In their own minds, they are all-knowing and all-powerful. They seem to treat their nurses, staff, and patients as if the world revolves around them and only them. Sadly, the days of the compassionate, selfless, and servant-hearted doctor seem to have been replaced by the self-absorbed, greedy, and career-driven physician. Altruism somehow got lost under growing stacks of paperwork and medical charts, and a doctor's home life has taken a backseat to the burning desire for bigger bank accounts and moving up the ladder of success.

I don't want to be one of these doctors, and I don't want you to be one of the these doctors either. That is why I poured my heart and soul into writing this Bible study. I'm not a biblical scholar or a world renowned, award-winning author. I never went to seminary, and I have never pastored a church. I'm just a simple E.R. doctor who loves Jesus, and my hope and prayer is that over the next several weeks, God's Holy Word will be a "lamp for your feet and a light for your path" (**Psalm 119:105**) that will help you to persevere down the road less traveled.

Let's get started! I tailored this study toward current or aspiring medical professionals (students, residents, doctors, dentists, etc.), more specifically young men (although I definitely feel that young women would greatly benefit from the study as well). Whether you are a seasoned veteran and biblical scholar or a rookie without a clue (see page 141 for a brief overview of the Gospel before starting the study if you feel like you fall into this category) who doesn't know whether Song of Solomon is a book in the Bible or a British rock band, you will undoubtedly be blessed by studying diligently through the pages that follow. The vast majority of what you will learn over the course of the next several weeks will not come from me but from the very words of God Himself as "all scripture is breathed out by God and profitable for teaching, for reproof, for correction, and for training in righteousness, that the man of God may be complete, equipped for every good work" (**2 Timothy 3:16-17, ESV**). My goal is not to give you my opinion on how to become a great Christian doctor; instead, I pray that through the inductive study of scripture, the Holy Spirit will unpack spiritual truths that will have an eternal impact on you, your family, your colleagues, and your patients.

If you've never done a formal Bible study, don't worry. I too remember feeling inadequate and overwhelmed the first time I decided to accept the challenge of of studying God's Word. I was in my second year of medical school when my friends Daniel and Tanner gave me a bad sales pitch and tried to convince me to do a Bible study on the book of Ephesians. It was a daily commitment, and we would meet once a week at 6:00 A.M. (I am the polar opposite of a morning person) to discuss what we learned. In my mind, time was scarce and I was trying to cram my brain full of pharmacology and pathology--I didn't have enough free time to eat, so I definitely didn't have time to do a Bible study, much less one that would require me to wake up while it was still dark outside. After much kicking and screaming, I begrudgingly agreed to participate, and looking back, it was a decision that changed my life. For the first time in my life, I made God a priority. While it may have seemed difficult at first, like most everything in life, I have found in the years since that studying the Word gets easier with discipline and practice. Michael Phelps didn't become the greatest swimmer of all time by floating down the lazy river every day; likewise, we can't be expected to live out God's Word unless we discipline ourselves to study scripture daily and have His Word written on our hearts (**Jeremiah 31:33**).

Your assignment for today is a simple one. First, if you don't already own a Bible, get one. I know that you are a poor (we will get to that in a few weeks) student or resident, but if you can afford to shell out tens of thousands of dollars in student loans to go to school and learn about medicine, buying one more book won't break the bank. If you already have a Bible, brush the dust off the cover because it is going to get put to good use over the coming weeks. Second, prayerfully commit to doing this study--doing so just might change your life. That is my prayer for you.

"Lord, I thank You for giving us the precious gift of Your Word. As Paul writes in 2 Thessalonians, I pray that over the coming weeks, You would direct our hearts to the love of God and to the steadfastness of Christ. Reveal to us through Your Word truths that will make an eternal impact for your kingdom. Allow me to decrease so that You may increase, and change my life so I can change the lives of others. Amen."

Day Two

In today's culture, it isn't easy to be a Christian physician. We are a dying breed, sitting on the endangered species list right between the bald eagle and the giant panda, but I'm confident that with God's help, we can make a comeback.

The world tells us that being a doctor is a glamorous profession. It's a field for the best and the brightest. Doctors on television and in the movies are smart, good-looking, rich, and powerful. Physicians top the list of America's most respected professions every year, and many of our country's most prestigious leaders have a background in medicine. Doctors seem to have it all.

It's easy to get caught up in this worldly mentality. I would be lying to myself if I didn't admit that for me, part of the draw to being a doctor was the money, job security, and respect that goes along with the title of M.D. But as believers, we have a higher calling. The American dream isn't necessarily God's dream for us.

"Do nothing from selfish ambition or conceit, but in humility count others more significant than yourselves."
(Philippians 2:3, ESV)

Seventy-five years ago, aspiring doctors lived by the second half of this verse. They were humble servants that went into medicine because they wanted to help people. Today, in our "me-first" culture, the first half of the verse is what resonates in the minds of most budding physicians. People now go into medicine because they want to drive a nice car and retire at a young age.

The only way to buck this cultural trend is by digging into scripture. Let's dissect two important passages over the next two days that will allow us to "shift our mindset to things that are above and not on things that are on earth" (**Colossians 3:2**).

Romans 12: 1-3 (ESV)

"I appeal to you therefore, brothers, by the mercies of God, to present your bodies as a living sacrifice, holy and acceptable to God, which is your spiritual worship. Do not be conformed to this world, but be transformed by the renewal of your mind, that by testing you may discern what is the will of God, what is good and acceptable and perfect. For by the grace given to me I say to everyone among you not to think of himself more highly than he ought to think, but to think with sober judgment, each according to the measure of faith that God has assigned."

Read through these three verses several times. Slowly meditate on each verse, first individually and then as a whole. Underline every verb so that you may fully grasp Paul's message as he is urging his fellow believers to action.

This may not come as a huge surprise to you, but the original Bible was not written in English. The Old Testament was predominantly written in Hebrew, and the New Testament was originally written in Greek. Over the centuries, these original texts have been translated into hundreds of different languages and versions, and while translators have done their best to accurately depict the message of the original texts, sometimes, the true meanings of words get "lost in translation." Therefore, it can be very beneficial for believers who are studying God's Word to go back to the original Greek text in order to glean insights we might otherwise miss by simply reading our English translations. Look up the Greek meanings of the following words from the passage you just read. If you have an expository dictionary (I would highly recommend *The Hebrew-Greek Key Word Study Bible* by Spiros Zodhiates), it will be a great tool for you to use going forward. If you don't have one, I like to use *blueletterbible.org*. It's free and easy to use, and it's a great resource to look up the meanings of words, cross-reference scripture, and compare different translations of the Word.

1. Appeal

2. Conformed

3. World

4. Transformed (Compare this use and context of the word to the same Greek word used in **Matthew 17:2** and and **Mark 9:2**)

5. Renewing

6. Mind

7. Prove

8. Will

Is your life a living sacrifice for God? Is the way you are living your spiritual worship? Are you currently a conformer that needs to be transformed? Do you think more highly of yourself than you ought? These are tough questions that we have to ask ourselves in order to become more like Jesus. Spend the next few minutes thinking of ways in which you currently conform to the patterns of the world and then consider some practical ways in which you can be transformed. I have left you ample space below. If you are a person that does better analyzing thoughts with charts, make a chart. If you are a lister, make a list. If you are a writer, write. Finally, spend some time in prayer and ask God to change your heart.

Day Three

"In the beginning was the Word, and the Word was with God, and the Word was God."
(John 1:1, ESV)

I've always thought that the Word of God gets short-changed by most Christians. I often hear Christians talking with reverence about the Holy Trinity (comprised of God, Christ, and the Holy Spirit), but rarely do I hear the Word of God receive its due respect. If the Word of God has been in existence since the beginning, and the Word *is* God and divinely inspired by God, I believe that it stands to reason that it should be of the utmost importance to God's people.

Look up and read the following four verses and pay special attention to verb tenses:

1) **John 1:14**

2) **Hebrews 4:12**

3) 1 Thessalonians 2:13

4) John 17:17

Did you note anything special about the Word of God in these four verses?

Now look up **Psalm 119:11**. As believers, what are we called to do with God's living Word?

I recently did a Bible study with my church entitled "The Mind of Christ" written by an incredible servant of God named T.W. Hunt. It was a fantastic study, and I would highly recommend it to anyone who wants to follow Jesus more closely. Just before Mr. Hunt died a few years ago, a couple of my friends went to listen to him preach in North Carolina after being overwhelmingly impressed by his teaching. When they asked him the secret to his unbelievable Christian faith, he simply responded "Love the Word." He could tell that this simple answer wasn't exactly the profound truth they were looking for so he expounded on his first answer by telling them that he loved the Word so much that he had read the entirety of the Bible in every single version the English language had to offer--all 77 of them! After they picked their jaws up off the floor, he went on to say with all humility that his love of God's Word was so vast that he chose to learn eight more languages for the sole purpose of being able to read the Bible in new ways. Needless to say, my friends left humbled with a new understanding of what it means to love God's Word. The meat of the "Mind of Christ" study was unpacking what it means to live out the 7 verses on the following page:

Philippians 2:5-11 (NKJV)

"Let this mind be in you which was also in Christ Jesus, who, being in the form of God, did not consider it robbery to be equal with God, but made Himself of no reputation, taking the form of a bondservant, and coming in the likeness of men. And being found in appearance as a man, He humbled Himself and became obedient to the point of death, even the death of the cross. Therefore God also has highly exalted Him and given Him the name which is above every name, that at the name of Jesus every knee should bow, of those in heaven, and of those on earth, and of those under the earth, and that every tongue should confess that Jesus Christ is Lord, to the glory of God the Father."

This is one of the most important foundational passages in the entire New Testament, so methodically read through these seven verses several times so you can fully grasp the impactful meaning of Paul's words. As Christians, we are called to imitate Christ, and these seven verses paint a very clear picture as to the humble attitude we must have in order to be more like Him.

Again, look up the Greek meanings of the following words from the passage above and note what you learn.

1) Form

2) Robbery

3) Equal

4) Bondservant

5) Humbled

6) Highly Exalted (note that this is the only time this Greek word is used in the entire Bible!)

Do you truly love the Word of God? Is the Word of God living and active in your life? Do you love God's Word so much that you are storing it up in your heart?

We can't be like Jesus until we first come to know and love God's Word. Every time that He faced a challenge or was forced to answer a difficult question, Jesus combatted the cultural conundrums He encountered from the world with scripture. His heart was so full of the Word that it couldn't help but overflow into His speech and His daily life. He could have chosen to say anything He wanted as He hung in agony on the cross, but the most important man in all of human history chose to quote scripture before He gave up His soul to God (**Matthew 27:46** and **Psalm 22**).

My challenge to you for today is to start storing up God's Word in your heart. Commit **Philippians 2:5-11** to memory. If you can memorize the Krebs cycle, you can memorize seven verses (I hate to burst your bubble, but despite what your professors tell you, you'll never see the Krebs cycle again after the test). Repeat these verses over and over again until they are ingrained into your memory. If you have a hard time memorizing scripture, try putting the words to a song (I learned this trick from my pastor's wife). It might sound silly at first, but making up a little jingle for a passage of scripture has really helped me to retain God's Word and commit it to my long-term memory.

Days Four and Five

Hopefully, by now God has your mind and your heart stirring a bit. We are only three days into our study, and you are already memorizing scripture and becoming proficient in Greek--give yourself a pat on the back! But if you are anything like me and you grew up entrenched in American culture, you probably won't be able to change the way you see the world or change the way you live within its confines quite as easily. Hearing God's Word is easy. Living it out is a different story, especially in the egocentric field of medicine.

As Christians, our primary responsibility in this life is to glorify God by living out our faith, but we can't do this on our own. Look up **Job 28:12-13** and record what you learn below.

Clearly, the only way that we can impact and change the culture amongst which we live is by seeking out answers from God's Word. Over the next two days, we are going to unpack several verses that will teach us how to change our hearts and practically live out the Gospel rather than live like the world. In the space below each verse or passage, write out your insights.

1) **2 Corinthians 5:17-21**

2) **Galatians 2:19-20**

3) **Galatians 6:14-15**

4) **Ephesians 4:17-24**

5) Matthew 16:24-25

6) Luke 14:33

7) 1 John 2:15-17

8) Colossians 2:8

9) Matthew 22:37-38

10) Philippians 2:3-4; Galatians 5:26 (note the Greek word for "conceit/conceited" along with its meaning)

11) 1 Corinthians 10:31

12) Matthew 6:33

13) James 1:22

14) Matthew 25:34-40

15) James 2:14-19

16) 1 John 2:4-6

17) Matthew 10:32-33

18) Revelation 3:15-18

Well done thy good and faithful servant! That may have seemed like a marathon of scripture, but it was a necessary race to run. Are you beginning to grasp the importance of the Word? Let's finish this first week of study in prayer:

"Thank You God for allowing me to make You a priority this week. Please allow Your Word to transform me. Please help me die to self and live for You. No longer allow me to go through the motions of life as a lukewarm believer, but help me to catch fire for Your cause. No longer allow me to seek after my own vain glory, but help me to seek Yours and Yours alone. Amen."

WEEK TWO

A CULTURE CHANGE, PART TWO

Day One

"There is but one just use of power, and it is to serve people."
         -George H.W. Bush

As a doctor in today's culture, God is going to give you both knowledge and power. People are constantly going to be coming to you for answers. My phone is frequently bombarded with pictures of pediatric rashes from friends and family members that for some reason unbeknownst to me think that I am a dermatologist. More importantly, you will be looked at as a leader in your clinic, department, or hospital. You will likely be called upon as a leader in your community as well.

You will deal with this responsibility of power in one of two ways. The majority of physicians in America allow power to go to their heads and attempt to use it for selfish gain. But as Christian physicians, we are called to follow the example of Christ and use our God-given gifts to serve others.

As a student, I quickly found that the emergency department was a perfect place for me display a servant's heart. For those of you that have never stepped foot in an E.R., it's a fascinating and magical place. It's filled with some of the most interesting characters known to the human race, many of which have burned every bridge and have been tossed to the curb by society. Most doctors disregard these outcasts for their terminal condition known as "insurance deficiency" rather than looking at them as human beings.

Jesus wouldn't have this attitude, and neither should we. Let's take a look at three passages in which Jesus addresses the subject of power. Record what you glean from Jesus' teachings in the space below.

1) John 13:1-16

2) **Matthew 20:16**

3) **Mark 10:42-45**

In **John 3:30**, John the Baptist gives one of the most simple yet beautifully profound statements ever spoken by man. Look it up and record it below.

My buddy Curt is one of the most incredible men of God that you could ever meet. God has given him many gifts, one of which is music. A few years back, he gave me a CD of songs that he had written (actually, he would tell you that God wrote them and he just sang them). One specific song really stood out to me because I thought it perfectly encapsulated the Christian journey of sanctification (**1 Thessalonians 4:3**) in which God transforms us from selfish children into selfless saints. At first, I thought that Curt had written it, but I subsequently learned that it was pirated--it was originally a hymn written by a man named Theodore Monod back in 1875. Curt's version is infinitely better than the original (no offense Mr. Monod), and the lyrics are as follows:

1. Oh, the bitter pain and sorrow

That a time could ever be,

When I proudly said to Jesus,

"All of self, and none of Thee."

All of self, and none of Thee,

All of self, and none of Thee,

When I proudly said to Jesus,

"All of self, and none of Thee."

2. Yet He found me; I beheld Him

Bleeding on th' accursed tree,

And my wistful heart said faintly,

"Some of self, and some of Thee."

Some of self, and some of Thee,

Some of self, and some of Thee,

And my wistful heart said faintly,

"Some of self, and some of Thee."

3. Day by day His tender mercy,

Healing, helping, full and free,

Brought me lower while I whispered,

"Less of self, and more of Thee."

Less of self, and more of Thee,

Less of self, and more or Thee,

Brought me lower while I whispered,

"Less of self, and more of Thee."

4. Higher than the highest heaven,

Deeper than the deepest sea,

Lord, Thy love at last has conquered:

"None of self, and all of Thee."

None of self, and all of Thee,

None of self, and all of Thee,

Lord, Thy love at last has conquered:

"None of self, and all of Thee."

These words may have been written more than a century ago, but they still ring true today. In order to fully embrace servanthood, we must first learn to empty ourselves. We must decrease, and He must increase. Close today in prayer, and ask God to give you the humble heart of a servant. Finally, during the course of this week, seek out ways to show humility and look for opportunities to serve others. Hopefully, doing so will help you develop habits that will last a lifetime.

Day Two

Have you ever heard the mantra, "Fake it 'til you make it"? It's easy to do in our culture. I can masquerade as a decent basketball player when I'm around other players that know how to play the game. I can sound like a competent singer when I have ten other people with beautiful voices singing alongside me. I can even pass for fashionable when my mother-in-law picks out my clothes.

But I can't fake it with God. He is both omnipotent (**Isaiah 44:24**) and omniscient (**Psalm 139 1-4**). He knows my every thought.

I have met several doctors who are good at "faking it." They put on their empathetic face and white coat of benevolence when they walk into work and then throw both in the backseat as they pull out of the parking lot. Others use compassionate words with their patients and then talk to their nurses, staff, and spouses with less respect than they show their dogs. Many physicians will give money to a cause only because it helps their business and gets their name in the newspaper.

Let's take a look at a few examples in which Jesus addresses such behavior. Read the following four passages and record what you learn from each example.

1) **Matt 23:1-12**

2) **Luke 18:10-14** (note the Greek word for "justified" along with its meaning)

3) **Isaiah 66:3-4 (NLT)**

4) **Philippians 3:17-21**

Now flip over a few chapters in your Bible and read **Galatians 1:10**. Write out the verse in the space below and answer the question as if Paul was there and asking it directly to you. Finally, commit this verse to memory so that it may serve as a constant reminder in guiding every big decision you will make for the rest of your life.

I would like to finish today with some very pertinent, wise words that I learned in medical school. I was on my internal medicine rotation during my third year when my group's attending physician enlightened my group with the following statement that has stuck with me ever since: "You can't polish a turd." His words couldn't be more true. No matter how hard you try to make it look pretty on the outside, you can't hide the fact that the shiny object you are trying to present as something that it's not is still, at its core, a turd. Repent. Don't allow yourself to be a polished turd.

Day Three

Now that we have clearly established the essentialness of a culture change for the Christian physician, let's spend today exploring how the world may respond. I'll give you a hint--it may not always be pretty. Standing up for Jesus in the medical field can be lonely. You will likely subject yourself to finger-pointing and ridicule as the majority of your colleagues probably won't share your beliefs. Let's take a look at several passages that paint a clearer picture as to the challenges we may expect to face as we live out our faith in the workplace. Record your insights from each passage that follows.

1) James 4:4

2) 1 John 3:13

3) 2 Timothy 3:10-13

4) Philippians 1:29-30

5) Matthew 5:10-12

6) Matthew 10:16-24

7) John 15:18-25

8) John 16:33 (note the Greek word for "tribulation" along with its meaning)

9) Mark 13:13

As believers, how are we to respond to such trials? Look up the following passages and note what you learn.

1) James 1:2-4

2)   1 Peter 1:6-9

3)   1 Peter 4:12-19

4)   1 Peter 5:8-10

5)   Romans 5:3-5

As followers of Jesus, we are promised affliction, persecution and suffering. It isn't a question of if--it's a question of when. But our suffering will not be in vain (**Romans 8:18**), and luckily, we don't have to face this inevitable truth alone. As we already learned, we have the living and active Word of God to help us combat the trials we are guaranteed to face. And as we will explore over the next two days, we also have another secret weapon at our disposal...

Days Four and Five

When I was three years old, I excitedly ran up to my parents one morning after Sunday school to tell them the most amazing thing that I had learned in class. This was a real game-changer. God wasn't just one person--He was actually three! I explained to them that each component of the Holy Trinity had a name. There was, "God the Father, Jesus the Son, and Holy the Ghost."

Until just a few years ago, my mind never really moved past my three year-old self's interpretation of "Holy the Ghost." I thought of the Holy Spirit, and in my mind, I saw "Casper." I didn't grasp that the same Spirit of God that allowed Him to create the heavens, the earth, and everything in existence (**Isaiah 66:2**) is still alive today. The same Spirit of God that allowed Jesus and His followers to perform extraordinary miracles here on earth lives inside of me. It's a hard concept to wrap our simple human minds around, but let's spend the next couple of days trying.

Look up the following two passages, and then answer the following questions. How long has the Holy Spirit been around? Was God alone when He created man? Pay special attention to pronouns.

1) **Genesis 1:1-2**

2) **Genesis 1:26**

The Holy Spirit wears many hats. He is an author, a comforter, a helper, an advocate, a counselor, a convictor, a down-payment, a guide, an intercessor, a resident, and a teacher (and this list just scratches the surface!). Not a bad resource to have living inside of you, huh? Let's dive into God's Word and explore the many important roles of the Holy Spirit.

Look up the following verses and record what you learn from each passage.

1) **2 Peter 1:21**

2) **John 14:16; John 14:26; John 15:26; John 16:7; 1 John 2:1**

Look up and record the Greek word for "helper/advocate," and record its definition below. Note that this word is used in only these five instances in the entire New Testament.

3) John 16:7-11

Look up the Greek word for "convict," and record its definition as well as what you learn from it below.

4) 2 Corinthians 1:22; 2 Corinthians 5:5; Ephesians 1:13-14

Look up and record the Greek word for "pledge/seal/guarantee," and record its definition and what you learn from it below.

5) John 16:13

Look up and record the Greek word for "guide," and record its definition and what you learn from it below.

6) Romans 8:9-11; 1 Corinthians 6:19; 1 John 4:1-6

7) **Romans 8:26**

Look up and record the Greek word for "intercedes," and record its definition and what you learn from it below. Note that this is the only time this word shows up in the New Testament.

8) **1 Corinthians 2:9-16**

9) Galatians 5:25

10) Ezekiel 36:26-27

When it comes to the Holy Spirit, I don't think that my simple mind will ever fully grasp just what an incredible and precious gift God has given to us as believers. It's a gift that is completely undeserved but one for which I am eternally grateful. As physicians, we don't have to change the culture in which we live and work alone--we have a helper. We have a guide and an advocate living inside of us that serves as a constant intercessor to God on our behalf, comforting us, convicting us, and teaching us how to humbly serve God and wholeheartedly follow Jesus. He is the down-payment for our salvation and the author of the most important book ever written. Let's close this week by committing **1 John 4:4** to memory and by thanking God that "greater is the One living inside of us than he who is living in the world."

WEEK THREE

FINDING YOUR NICHE

Day One

When I started medical school, I was still unsure as to what I wanted to be when I grew up. There were so many specialties to choose from. I had always loved sports, so orthopedics or sports medicine was a strong possibility. I found the heart fascinating, so cardiology was quite high on my list. I had always been a magnet for kids, so pediatrics was appealing as well. With so many choices, I didn't know how I was going to make such an important decision. Luckily, one of my classmates showed me the chart on the following page:

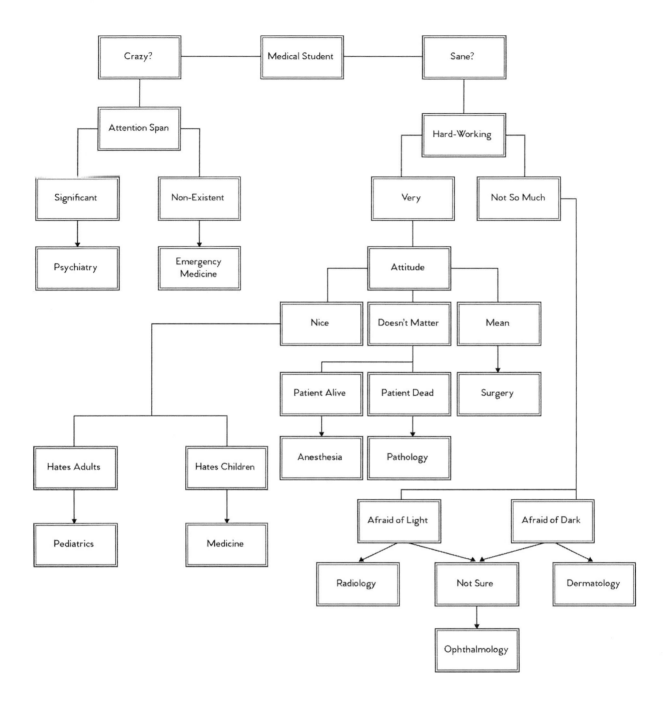

Aspiring physicians have many ways of picking a specialty. Some use "can't miss" flowcharts like the one above. Others use online quizzes or aptitude tests. Many base their big decision on "lifestyle" factors. But most students simply gravitate toward the one specialty that just "feels right." For me, that specialty was emergency medicine. When I walked into the E.R., I knew I had found my niche. It was chaotic. It was fast-paced. There was no "rounding." I never had to be "on call." It allowed me to learn about all fields of medicine without boxing me into one specific area of expertise. And when I realized that going into emergency medicine would essentially allow me to wear pajamas to work for the rest of my life, I was sold!

Looking back, I feel like I chose wisely. I can honestly say that I enjoy what I do, and I can't envision myself thriving in any other medical environment quite like I do in the E.R. However, when I remember back to the selection process, I am ashamed to admit how little a role I allowed God to play in such an important decision. I don't want you to make the same mistake.

Over the next week, we are going to explore what God's Word tells us regarding choosing and pursuing a career. What are your spiritual gifts? How can your talents best be used for the Kingdom? Where is God calling you to practice? These are just a few of the questions that we will attempt to address as we seek out answers from scripture.

Let's start this process by examining a few important verses:

1) 1 Corinthians 10:31

2) 1 Corinthians 15:58

3) Proverbs 3:5-8

4) Psalm 32:8

5) **Ecclesiastes 9:10**

Based on these verses, what should our attitudes be toward our work? How are we to decide what career path to pursue? Is it a decision that we are to make alone?

The medical professional has a lot of big decisions to make. Where should I go to medical school? Which specialty should I choose? Where should I go to residency? Should I do a fellowship? Where do I want to practice when I'm finally through with my training? When answering these important questions, we should always keep in mind that as believers, we should never lean on our own understanding. Seek God's helping hand: "Ask, and it will be given to you; seek, and you will find; knock, and it will be opened to you." (**Matthew 7:7, ESV**)

Day Two

If you grew up going to church like I did, there are probably specific words in the English language that you would consider "churchy." These are the words that you would only hear on Sundays but would then magically disappear from all vernacular throughout the other six days of the week. These are the words that you heard the preacher say but never really understood what they meant. Words like "grace, glory, and reconcile" immediately come to mind.

For me, the term "spiritual gift" fits into this category. Growing up, I never really understood what a spiritual gift actually was, so I certainly didn't know how to use one. For all I knew, my spiritual gift was probably sitting in a closet in an unopened box somewhere in the basement of my church.

Thankfully, I am no longer in the dark on this matter. Look up the Greek word for "gift" in **1 Corinthians 12:4**. Record its definition below. What do you learn about spiritual gifts from this definition? Where do they come from? Can they be earned?

There are four main passages in the New Testament pertaining to spiritual gifts, and each one is listed below. Read through each passage carefully, and record what you learn in the space provided. Additionally, at the end of today's lesson is a blank chart entitled "Spiritual Gifts." In the left hand column, number and list each spiritual gift that you note when searching through these verses. Be thorough--you will be using this list for the next two days as well.

1) **Romans 12:3-8**

2) **1 Peter 4:10-11**

3) **Ephesians 4:11-12**

4) **1 Corinthians 12**

Based on these passages, have all believers been given the same spiritual gifts?

What is God's purpose for giving us spiritual gifts? How are we to use them?

Day Three

Now that you have listed each of God's spiritual gifts, let's get practical. In the second column of the chart you started yesterday, record the Greek word and its definition of each spiritual gift from the text. You may note some redundancy, but don't take shortcuts. Take a few minutes and ponder over your list and definitions. Do you feel like any of these gifts apply specifically to you? Circle or underline these gifts, and in the space provided below, write out some practical ways that you could use each. How do your specific spiritual gifts apply to a career in medicine? Are there certain areas of medicine that your God-bestowed spiritual gifts would make you more suited for?

Day Four

"Talent is God-given. Be humble.

Fame is man-given. Be grateful.

Conceit is self-given. Be careful."

     -John Wooden

This famous quote from the late Coach Wooden may have originally been directed toward his young, impressionable college basketball players, but his words are a perfect reminder for both aspiring and practicing doctors as well.

As believers, God provides us with spiritual gifts, but He also gives us talents. Look up the word "talent" in a dictionary, and record its definition below:

How does this definition differ from the definition of "spiritual gift" that you noted on Day 2?

There is definitely overlap between the terms "talents" and "spiritual gifts," but they are clearly not one and the same. There are important distinctions to make between these two similar but different terms. Talents are natural. Spiritual gifts are supernatural. Talents are inherited from our parents and honed by training. Spiritual gifts are inherited from the Holy Spirit and honed by the Holy Spirit. Talents are possessed by both believers and unbelievers. Spiritual gifts are possessed exclusively by believers. Talents can be used selfishly. Spiritual gifts are used for God's glory to produce spiritual fruit (**Galatians 5:22-23**).

Don't get me wrong--a talent is a good thing. Talents are God-given, and discovering and developing them is essential for edifying the full and complete body of Christ. However, our talents should not be wasted for selfish gain.

Take a few minutes to list some of your God-given talents in the space provided on the following page. Don't short-change yourself by trying to be humble here--your talents ultimately come from God, so you can't take credit for them anyway.

Finally, compare the list of your God-given talents with your list of God-given spiritual gifts. As believers, it is essential that our talents and our spiritual gifts have a symbiotic relationship. Do you see any overlap between your lists? Do you see any patterns? How can you best use both of these precious gifts together to bring God the most glory? More specifically, is there a particular area of medicine where your talents and spiritual gifts might shine the brightest?

Day Five

As a medical student, I thought that once I had settled on a specialty, it would be smooth sailing. The hard decisions were over, right?

Wrong. The decisions were just starting to begin. You will face the same myriad of questions that I did a few short years ago. Where will I do my residency? Inpatient or outpatient? Academics or community? Do I join an existing group or start my own practice? Why didn't I have a single lecture in medical school about the business side of medicine? Do I want to practice in America or abroad?

When it comes to finding answers to these questions, my only advice would be to seek God.

My wife (a former math teacher) thought she had the answer key to the residency question. She came up with a scoring system (1-100), and after each interview, we sat down with our spreadsheets and assigned a score to each program that was weighted based on several categories (the city, the vibe I got from the residents, benefits, churches, distance from family, etc.) that we deemed most important. It was a great idea, but by the end of the interview process, I felt an overwhelming peace that this really wasn't our decision. Spreadsheets aside, God was going to put us where He wanted us to be. That became our prayer: "God, please put us where we can have the biggest impact for your Kingdom." I truly feel that He answered that prayer, and we had a wonderful and fruitful three years in Charleston, SC while I completed my training. The "Holy City" (as it is known to locals) was a holier place when we left than it was when we got there.

Choosing where to practice after residency may present an even more daunting challenge. Emergency medicine physicians are in high demand right now. Due to our current healthcare climate in America, many places are in desperate need of physicians and are throwing around exorbitant amounts of money at graduating residents in hopes of staffing their emergency departments. I literally could have gone anywhere to start practicing out of residency. However, I didn't choose my first job based on money, benefits, or a great 401K plan. I chose my first job because I felt a strong calling back to our church in Kentucky. My primary job in life is to live for Christ and lead my wife and children to an eternal home in heaven. My secondary job is to be a doctor. The incredible group of men that I had come to know and love at our small church in Kentucky before I left for residency will never let me lose sight of this truth. The families that I have the privilege of worshipping God with truly love the Lord with all their heart, soul, mind and strength (**Luke 10:27**). I have no doubt in my mind that if something were to happen to me or my wife, I would trust every single man in my church to raise my children to know and follow Jesus. This relationship with our church is priceless, and ultimately, it's why we left the beaches of Charleston and moved back to Kentucky. You can't take a signing bonus or a beach house with you to heaven.

Read the following two verses and note what you learn below each.

1) **Proverbs 27:17**

2) **Ecclesiastes 4:12**

Based on these verses, how important is it to surround yourself with other like-minded believers?

Take a look back at your list of talents and spiritual gifts. Do you have a gift for teaching? Maybe God is pointing you toward a career in academic medicine. Do you have a gift for serving? Perhaps you would be more suited for a job in the community. Do you have a gift for leadership or administration? Maybe you would make a great medical director. Do you speak other languages or have a heart for missions? Maybe God is directing you toward an opportunity somewhere overseas. What setting are your talents and spiritual gifts most suited for? Why do you feel that way? Where can you have the greatest impact for God's Kingdom? List your thoughts below, and then spend some time in prayer.

Finally, look up the following three verses, and record what you learn from each. How do these verses apply to working as a physician?

1) **Matthew 5:16**

2) **Matthew 28:18-20**

3) **Luke 5:31**

Let's close this week in prayer:

"Lord, thank You for giving me talents. Thank You for my spiritual gifts. Please help me to maximize them to make the greatest impact for Your Kingdom. Direct me in the path You want me to go. Lead me to seek Your will. Surround me with believers that will sharpen me and challenge me to be more like Jesus. Allow me to use my job as a means to let my light shine before men and to make disciples for You. Amen."

WEEK FOUR

MORE MONEY, MORE PROBLEMS?, PART ONE

Day One

"For the love of money is the root of all kinds of evil. And some people, craving money, have wandered from the true faith and pierced themselves with many sorrows."

--1 Timothy 6:10 (NLT)

We all come from different financial upbringings. Maybe you grew up in an affluent family, or maybe your family lived from paycheck to paycheck. Perhaps you grew up like me, smack dab in the center of the American middle class. No matter your monetary background, the verse above is about to become far more pertinent to you in the coming years.

I know exactly what you are thinking right now. I'm a poor student. I essentially make minimum wage as a resident. I'm up to my neck in debt with student loans. You may feel that way, but the truth of the matter is that nearly half of the world's population lives on less than $2 per day. Therefore, the average medical resident's salary in America is more than one hundred times that of the average human on planet earth. You are far more blessed than you may realize.

Lean in, listen closely, and let me share an earth-shattering secret with you. As a doctor in America, you are going to make a lot of money. It doesn't matter if you go into primary care or plastic surgery--in comparison to the rest of the world (and most of America), you will be considered wealthy. This is an inevitable truth and an undebatable fact. However, the importance of your attitude toward money and how you choose to use it cannot be understated.

God isn't silent when it comes to the subject of money. Nearly half of all of Jesus' parables deal with the subject of money. There are more than twice as many verses in scripture about money than there are about faith and prayer.

We learn from Paul in **Colossians 4:14** that his beloved friend Luke (the author of the books of Luke and Acts) is a physician. I find it both ironic and appropriate that Dr. Luke writes more about finances in his gospel account than do the authors of the other three gospels. I don't know what the going salary was for a physician in the first century, but Luke must have had enough money to grasp its impactful effect on those to whom he was writing.

Over the next two weeks, we are going to examine what God's Word tells us about money. Allow scripture to be your financial foundation, and consider God your financial advisor as you explore the purpose of money in the life of a believer. Read the following four verses and record what you learn from each in the space provided.

1) **Psalm 24:1**

2) **Colossians 1:16**

3) **James 1:17**

4) **1 Chronicles 29:13-16**

Based on these verses, where does our money come from? To whom does all money ultimately belong?

Keep the answers to these questions in mind as you seek out biblical answers to your financial questions in the coming days.

As a physician, God has given you a great responsibility when it comes to money. Remember Dr. Luke's words as we march forward in our study over the next two weeks: "When someone has been given much, much will be required in return; and when someone has been entrusted with much, even more will be required" (**Luke 12:48, NLT**).

Days Two and Three

Over the next two days, we are going to dive into a few passages in the New Testament regarding how some specific biblical characters handled their money. Note the size of each person's bank account, and pay close attention to each individual's actions regarding their finances. As you look up each passage, there are a few questions you should attempt to answer. Who are the main characters in the passage? How did these characters view money? What was their attitude toward their money? What was the result of their attitude/actions? How would I have acted had I been in their shoes? What lessons can you learn from these case studies that will allow you to make some practical changes in the way you view money? Answer these questions, and note any other insights that you glean from each passage in the space provided below.

1) **Luke 21:1-4**

2) **Luke 18:18-25**

3) Mark 10:17-27

4) Luke 19:11-27

5) Acts 5:1-11

6) Luke 19:1-10

Days Four and Five

"What good is it for a man to gain the whole world, yet forfeit his soul?"

--Mark 8:36 (NIV)

I'm sure you have heard the old saying "attitude is everything." When it comes to the subject of money, this adage couldn't be any more telling. Our attitude toward money paints a clear picture of who we are (or who we are pretending to be) to the world around us. If you want insight into a person's soul, look no further than their checkbook, for "where your treasure is, there your heart will be also" **(Matthew 6:21, NIV).**

Look up the NLT version of **Philippians 2:5**. This verse should be quite familiar to you as you memorized it several weeks ago. Based on this verse, after whom should we pattern our attitude?

As believers, our attitude toward money should look like that of Christ's. This is no easy task as Jesus set the bar quite high. Sometimes, with the aid of the Holy Spirit, we are able to joyfully follow Jesus' example with our money, but other times, our selfishness shines through, and we fall short. Allow me to give you two personal examples.

When I started my residency in Charleston, SC, my wife (Amanda) was split between two job opportunities. The first was a teaching job at a public school that would pay her nearly $40,000 per year. The second was at a small, private Christian school and paid only $18,000 per year. At the time, it was still just Amanda and me. We were kidless. We knew that we wanted to start a family, but we were concerned that we wouldn't be able to afford a baby. We also knew that once we had a baby, Amanda would stop teaching and stay at home to be a full-time mom. Conventional wisdom told us to take the public school job, but I felt strongly that Amanda was to take the job at the Christian school. After much prayer, she decided to open door number two and took the job at the Christian school, and the Lord honored our decision. He allowed her to develop incredible, life-long relationships with her co-workers and the mothers of her students that allowed her to grow in her faith and helped better equip and prepare her for motherhood. By going against the grain, she was able to have a far greater impact for God's Kingdom than she ever could have had she chosen to take the higher paying job. But God didn't stop there. After unsuccessfully trying to get pregnant for months, we finally conceived on the **exact same day** that I signed a contract to come back to Kentucky after residency. As part of my contract, I received a $36,000 signing bonus that paid me a monthly stipend over my final two years of residency. Do the math. My signing bonus literally replaced Amanda's salary to the dollar. Only God could have orchestrated such a story.

Conversely, this past summer, I asked my employer for a raise. I wrote an elaborate email, eloquently explaining why I felt like a raise was warranted. I outlined my case perfectly. My Press Ganey scores were off the charts. I had recruited other physicians and medical providers to our hospital. I had produced more RVUs (saw more patients and made more money for our employer) than any other physician in our group. I had several lucrative offers from other hospitals in the area that were actively recruiting me. There is no way that they would say no, right? Wrong. I got denied. My natural human response was to "stick it to the man" and leave. However, when I examined my heart, I realized that my motives for asking for more money were both selfish and prideful. Simply put, I had the wrong attitude.

We are going to spend the next two days examining our attitude toward money. As you look up and meditate on the passages on the next page, answer the following questions. Who is speaking, and to whom are they speaking? What is my current attitude toward money (be honest with yourself--God knows your heart)? What should our attitude be toward money? To whom should our money go? How can I apply this passage to my own life?

1) Matthew 6:24

2) Hebrews 13:5

3) 1 Timothy 6:6-12

4) Philippians 4:10-14

5) Romans 13:1-8

6) 1 John 2:15-17

7) 1 John 3:16-18

8) Acts 2:41-45

9) Acts 4:32-35

10) Jeremiah 17:9-11

11) Jeremiah 9:23-24

12) Psalm 119:14

What is your current attitude toward money? Is it something that consumes you? Is it constantly on your mind? Is it something that you frequently worry about? Spend a few minutes below recording your current thoughts, fears and goals when it comes to money. If you need to repent, it's okay.

Let's close this week in prayer:

"Lord, thank You for blessing me with more money than I will ever need. Allow me to fully understand that everything I have comes from You. Help me to emulate the attitude of Jesus, not just with my money, but in all that I do. Just as King David wrote in **Psalm 86**, "Teach me Your ways, O Lord, that I may live according to Your truth. Grant me purity of heart, so that I may honor You." Amen."

WEEK FIVE

MORE MONEY, MORE PROBLEMS?, PART TWO

Day One

Today, we are going to do a case study on the book of Ecclesiastes. This Old Testament book was written by King David's son, Solomon. In case you are unfamiliar with Solomon, allow me to quickly bring you up to speed on his financial background. King Solomon was born into royalty in Israel. He was the son of David and Bathsheba and the heir to David's throne. Early in young Solomon's reign, the Lord appeared to him in a dream (**1 Kings 3**) and asked Solomon, "What shall I give you?" Solomon responded by asking for wisdom, and this humble answer was very pleasing to God. God responded by not only giving Solomon unmatched wisdom but also by providing him with unmatched wealth. According to **1 Kings 10:23 (NIV)**, "King Solomon was greater in riches and wisdom than all the other kings of the earth." When you Google "richest man who ever lived," King Solomon's name frequently is mentioned at the top of most lists with an estimated current day net worth ranging from $100 billion to $2.1 trillion dollars. Needless to say, King Solomon knew a thing or two about money.

I would think that the wisest and richest man in human history would likely have some important wisdom to share when it comes to the subject of money. Read the following two passages and note what you learn.

1) **Ecclesiastes 2**

2) **Ecclesiastes 5:10-16**

As a physician, you will never have quite the riches and fortunes that King Solomon possessed, but you will have far more than most. Based on his advice, how much importance should you place on your wealth? What should your attitude be toward money?

Solomon spends the entire book of **Ecclesiastes** pondering how one can find contentment and fulfillment in life. He makes a case for wealth, achievement, success, material possessions, wisdom, obtaining knowledge, and several other human endeavors. Ultimately, he comes to his final conclusion in **Ecclesiastes 12:13**. Read this verse, and note what what you learn from it below. How can you apply his conclusion to your life as a physician?

Day Two

My wife and I have been married for seven years, so we have been on our fair share of dates. We have been to several unbelievable restaurants, we have had a few exciting weekend getaways, and we are constantly trying to outdo one another with surprises. However, if you were to ask either one of us about our most memorable date, we would undoubtedly give you the same answer.

We got married in between my second and third years of medical school. At the time, Amanda was our sole source of income and worked as a middle school math teacher to support us. We lived on a pretty tight budget, so when we went out to dinner, it was usually a pretty special occasion.

On one of our rare date nights, I decided to "splurge" and take Amanda to one of her favorite restaurants--Logan's Roadhouse. After a few baskets of rolls, a bucket of peanuts, and a wonderful meal, I asked the waiter to bring us the check. You should have seen the look on our faces when he proceeded to tell us that our meal was free. A random stranger in the restaurant had paid for our dinner. We were flabbergasted. We walked out of the restaurant, hand in hand, looking around for someone to thank, but the stranger that picked up our tab still remains a mystery to this day.

It still brings tears of joy to my eyes every time I reminisce about that date. The stranger that paid for our meal will never know the impact that they had on us that night. Their random act of kindness inspired us for a lifetime, and we now have the opportunity to do the same for other unsuspecting young couples.

We are going to take a more in depth look at giving and tithing in a few weeks, but before we do, let's explore a few verses that deal with the subject of giving. Note what each of the following passages teaches you about giving. What should our attitudes be like when it comes to giving?

1) **Acts 20:35**

2) **Luke 12:15**

3) Luke 12:33-34

4) Matthew 6:1-4

5) Deuteronomy 15:10

Day Three

Today, we are going to tackle a subject that I am sure is near and dear to your heart. It's a word that strikes fear in the psyche of every medical student in America. It's not "exam." It's not "boards." It's not "pimping." It's not "on call." It's worse.

Debt. You just cringed, didn't you? As the cost of a medical education continues to rise, so do the mountains of debt that students are forced to overcome following graduation. When I finished medical school, I faced the unenviable task of paying back more than $170,000 in student loans--and compared to a lot of my classmates, that figure was pretty cheap.

Debt isn't just limited to tuition. Perhaps you owe money on a house or a car. Maybe you have credit card debt or have undergraduate loans to pay back as well. I watched my parents struggle with debt for decades, and their poor spending habits ultimately led to them being forced into declaring bankruptcy. I don't want you to ever be in the same boat.

The Bible has much to say regarding the subject of debt. According to **2 Peter 2:19 (NLT)**, "you are a slave to whatever controls you." Read **Proverbs 22:7**. Based on these two verses, what conclusions can you draw regarding debt?

Use the space below to list your current debts. Include what the debt is for as well as the amount.

Now look up the following two verses and record your insights below. What do you learn from these passages regarding spending habits and debt? How can you practically apply these verses to your current financial situation?

1) Luke 14:28-30

2) Romans 13:8

Paying back your student loans may seem like an impossible, uphill climb at this point in your life. I felt the same way when I was in your shoes. However, by making responsible financial decisions and living within our means, God allowed my wife and I to erase all of my student loans within two years of finishing residency. With the right attitude toward money, you will be able to do the same. Here are a few practical tips that we employed that you might find helpful in reducing, avoiding, and eliminating your debt:

1) Don't buy something (aside from a house) unless you can pay for it with cash.
2) Consider refinancing or consolidating your student loans. I refinanced my student loans after finishing residency, and my interest rate dropped nearly 5%.
3) When purchasing a home, opt for a 15 year (or less) mortgage. If you need 30 years to pay off a house, it is probably more house than you will ever need.
4) Create a budget during residency and stick to it. You need to know where all of your money is going so that it isn't being wasted.
5) Use coupons! During residency, Amanda was nearly able to slice our grocery budget in half by learning how to take advantage of coupon deals.
6) After finishing residency, continue to live on your residency budget afterward. Use your surplus to aggressively pay off your debt.

Finally, remember that Jesus knows more about debt than anyone in human history. Read **1 Timothy 2:6** and note what you learn.

Jesus gave his life to purchase freedom for everyone in human history. He paid the entire debt of all of humanity. When you try to wrap your mind around that truth, your student loans will feel like peanuts in comparison.

Day Four

Now that we better understand debt, we are going to use today to explore the opposite end of the money spectrum and study what God's Word tells us about saving and investing. You may not have the means to do much saving right now, but you soon will. When that opportunity comes, it is very important that you are well versed on scripture.

Read **Proverbs 21:20**. Look up the Hebrew transliterations for the words "treasure" and "swallow" (note that the Hebrew word for "swallow" is the same word used in **Jonah 1:17** when he is swallowed by the whale). Note what you learn from the verse and these words on the following page.

Now look up **1 Timothy 6:17-19**, and record your insights. Record the Greek word for "storing up" as well as what you learn from its definition.

It is clear from these verses and others (remember back to Jesus' parable of the minas in **Luke 19**) that God has called us to be good stewards of the money He has blessed us with, and that there is an important place for saving and investing. However, there is a fine line between investing responsibly as a foundation for the future and selfishly hoarding our money for ourselves.

Read the following passages and record your insights below.

1) **Luke 12:16-21**

2) **Matthew 6:19-24**

3) **James 5:1-5**

4) **2 Corinthians 12:14-15**

In my humble opinion, investing and saving seems to be a matter of the heart. If your attitude is like that of Christ's, you understand that the money that you are storing up for the future is not for you anyway. It belongs to God, and you will multiply and use it for His glory. If your attitude is like that of the world, and you are selfishly stockpiling your money for yourself so you can retire early and spend your golden years wasting away and sipping piña coladas at your condo by the beach, you have probably missed the mark. Ultimately, our most important investments in this life have nothing to do with money. As Christians, we are called to invest in the lives of others, and this investment in eternity is where we should be placing our time and our effort. I have never seen a U-Haul truck attached to the back of a casket at a funeral, and Roth IRAs don't rollover to heaven.

God provides us with a wonderful illustration of saving and investing through nature. Let's examine two of God's creatures--the ant and the bear. Ants are fascinating creatures. They never stop working, and they always seem to be thinking one step ahead. They are constantly gathering and storing up food for times of need. God even compliments the ant's work ethic in **Proverbs 6:6** and **Proverbs 30.25**. Bears, however, are a different story. When you really think about it, bears are quite selfish. They are lazy, gluttonous creatures that hoard up food for themselves so that they can sleep for months. Interestingly enough, there are no complimentary proverbs about the bear's work ethic and saving habits. Don't hoard your money, and don't waste your life. Don't be a bear. Be an ant.

Day Five

Let's close this week by exploring a few words of wisdom from Psalms and Proverbs. These invaluable books of the Bible provide us with poems, songs of worship, and practical advice for the life of a believer. They also have a great deal to teach us about money. Look up the following verses and note what you learn in the space provided.

1) Proverbs 3:9-10

2) Proverbs 21:17

3) Proverbs 13:11

4) Proverbs 22:2

5) Proverbs 11:28

6) Proverbs 23:4-5

7) Psalm 34:10

8) **Psalm 52:7**

9) **Psalm 49:20**

Well done! You just completed your crash course in biblical finance 101. I pray that these past two weeks have been beneficial, and that your heart has been stirred by the Holy Spirit. Take a few minutes, and record what God has revealed to you over the past two weeks regarding money. Summarize the points that stuck out to you most, and list some practical ways that your newfound attitude toward money will shape the way you use God's money going forward.

Let's close our week in prayer:

"Thank You Lord for providing us with far more than we will ever need. Give us wisdom. Help us to be good stewards of the money You have so richly blessed us with. Allow us not to be consumed by money or the material things of this world, but instead, lift our eyes toward heaven. Amen."

WEEK SIX

WITNESS WHILE YOU WORK, PART ONE

Day One

"Whatever your hand finds to do, do it with all your might..."
   --**Ecclesiastes 9:10 (ESV)**

As a budding physician, I'm sure that you are quite familiar with hard work. Getting into medical school is no easy task and requires sacrifice, diligence, and discipline. Medical school is a lengthy, four year grind, and residency can feel like both an overwhelming and unrelenting marathon. Your long, arduous struggle toward your M.D. will sometimes leave you feeling exhausted, sleep-deprived, over-worked, and wondering why you didn't simply pick a job in which you could sit at a desk from 9 A.M. to 5 P.M. and actually experience a real lunch break.

Work is an integral part of the Christian faith. We learn from the book of James that "faith without works is dead" (**James 2:26**), and that we are to be "doers of the word and not hearers only"(**James 1:22**). We can't work our way to heaven, but as believers, God crafted us for work.

God has given man several important earthly roles, all of which pertain to work. We will discuss these roles in greater detail in a few more weeks, so consider today your shrimp cocktail. God made man to be a leader (**1 Corinthians 11:3**), a provider (**1 Timothy 5:8**), and a worker (**Genesis 2:15-20**). Today, we will focus on the latter of these.

Look up **Genesis 2:15-20**, and record your insights regarding work below.

Look up the Hebrew word for "work" in verse 15. Record its definition.

What was Adam's original job(s)?

Did God give these jobs to Adam before or after the fall of man? Was work an institution created by God for man from the beginning, or was it a punishment that resulted from the fall? Why do you feel that way?

However, God clearly established the importance of work even before he created Adam. He showed us through creation that He wasn't above working Himself. Read **Genesis 1**, and use the space provided to record what you learn about God's attitude toward work.

Jesus wasn't above working either--He actually embraced it! Look up **Mark 6:1-3** and John **14:1-3,** and note any insights you glean regarding the work of Christ.

Work shouldn't be a burden to believers--it should be a blessing. It provides us with an opportunity to serve the God that created us in His image and a chance for us to follow in the footsteps of Jesus. Let us close today in prayer, and ask Him to transform our worldview on work over the next two weeks:

"Lord, we thank You for the gift of work. Allow us to be diligent workers for Your Kingdom and to embrace work with a zealous and joyful heart. Help us to view work as an opportunity to make You known. As You spoke through Paul in **1 Corinthians 16**, allow us to be strong and courageous men, and let all the work that we do for You be done in love. Amen."

Day Two

Today, we are going to do four case studies in order to take a deeper dive into the subject of work. As you read through each passage, meditate on its message, and answer the questions that follow.

1) **Genesis 6:11-7:5**

How did Noah respond to God's command?

What were some alternate responses he could have shown God?

What can you learn from Noah's actions, obedience, and attitude that you can apply to your own life when it comes to the subject of work?

2) Genesis 29:1-28

What was Jacob's attitude toward work?

How did Jacob respond to being treated unfairly by Laban?

Have you ever been wronged or short-changed after working hard? How did you respond? In lieu of what you learned from Jacob, how might you respond differently when you face your next work conflict?

3) Ezra 1; Ezra 2:64-Ezra 3

How did the people of Israel respond to King Cyrus' challenge?

What can we learn from their attitude and their willingness to work and give abundantly?

4) Matthew 25:14-30

How did each of the three servants respond to the task they were given by their master?

What insights can you glean from this parable when it comes to laziness?

Days Three and Four

The Bible has much to tell us about how believers are to be diligent workers. It also warns us against laziness. Over the next two days, we are going to unpack several verses and learn specifics about how God calls us to view our work. As you read through all of these passages, consider how each verse pertains to your work as a physician.

1) **Romans 12:11-12**

2) **Colossians 3:23-24**

3) **Proverbs 16:3**

4) **Ephesians 5:15-16**

5) Psalm 128:2

6) Galatians 6:4

7) 2 Timothy 2:6

8) 2 Timothy 2:15

9) Ephesians 2:8-10

10) 2 Thessalonians 3:6-12

11) Proverbs 13:4

12) Proverbs 14:23

13) Proverbs 21:25

14) Proverbs 10:4

15) Philippians 2:14-16

Reading through these passages reminds me of Caleb, one of my favorite men in all of the Bible. In case you are unfamiliar with Caleb, allow me to give you a brief synopsis of his character. We are introduced to Caleb in the book of Numbers in the Old Testament. After the rescued nation of Israel walks across the parted Red Sea following their deliverance out of Egypt, Caleb (along with Joshua) is one of the twelve men that Moses selects to go spy out and explore the promised land (the land of Canaan that was promised to

Abraham and his descendents centuries before). After forty days of exploring, the group of spies returns to Moses and the Israelite people with their report of the land. While the spies agreed that the land was bountiful and good, ten of the twelve men were terrified to proceed toward the promised land because it was inhabited by strong, giant warriors called Anakim that these men felt would be impossible for the Israelites to defeat. Only Caleb and Joshua had faith that God would deliver on His promise to bring the Israelites into Canaan. Read **Numbers 13:25-30**, and note what you learn about Caleb from his response below.

Despite Caleb and Joshua's best attempt to convince the Israelites otherwise, fear won over, and the cries of Caleb and Joshua were drowned out by the faithless majority. God chooses to punish the Israelites' lack of faith by forcing them to wander through the wilderness for forty years before entering the promised land so that all of those over the age of twenty who did not have faith would die prior to Him delivering on His promise. All the while, Caleb and Joshua continue to be faithful and diligent workers for the Lord without grumbling or complaining, and ultimately, their hard work and faith are rewarded as they are the only two people of the entire original generation of Israelites that crossed the Red Sea that God chooses to save, and He allows them to enter the promised land. Caleb's story culminates in **Joshua 14** when he is finally given his long-awaited inheritance after decades of faithful work. Read **Joshua 14:6-14**, note what you learn, and answer the questions that follow.

What do you learn about Caleb's attitude from this passage? Does he seem to hold a grudge toward God for making him wait forty-five years before receiving his inheritance?

How old is Caleb at this point?

What do you learn about Caleb from verses 11 and 12?

Do you now understand why I love Caleb? He is a fearless warrior of God, and his attitude is unwavering. He works diligently and faithfully for decades. At the end of his journey, he declares that he is still as strong as he was forty-five years earlier, and that he is ready for battle. The mental picture of an eighty-five year-old man still eager to take on an army of giants is so inspiring that it leaves me smiling every time I think about it. Caleb is a man that has the right attitude toward work. I can't imagine walking into the E.R. for a shift at the age of eighty-five with the same pep in my step that I have today, but if I can learn to embrace work with the same attitude as Caleb and allow him to be my role model, perhaps one day in 2069, I will.

Day Five

Over the past four days, we have clearly established the importance of work in the life of a believer. However, we can never allow our work to consume us. As a Christian physician, there is a fine line between working hard and overworking. While God calls us to be diligent workers, our work should never come at the expense of our relationships with our family and our fellow brothers and sisters in Christ. When I die, I don't want to be defined by my work as a physician. I want to be remembered as a faithful husband, loving father, and devoted man of God who led by example and happened to work as a physician.

I recently attended a national medical director's conference, and it was an eye opening experience for me. The men that I met with are well-known leaders in the field of emergency medicine, and through the lens of our culture, these doctors would be deemed quite successful. Some of them are at the top of my profession. However, when I began talking with them about their home lives, several mentioned that they were divorced while others were giving me advice on specific stores to visit before returning home in order to "buy" the love of my wife and children. I left the conference feeling broken-hearted for these men and their families and blessed that I had a Godly perspective on work.

I learned about the importance of balancing work and home life from my dad. My dad is a basketball coach, and he spent the majority of his career coaching at small colleges. He was always looking for a bigger and better opportunity, so my family frequently moved as he attempted to move up the coaching ranks. To this day, when someone asks me my hometown, I just shrug my shoulders.

My dad took his coaching job seriously, and he worked hard year after year to produce a winner on the court. Winning took sacrifice. He spent countless hours on the road recruiting, and he often spent his own money to recruit due to his limited budget. He poured his life into the lives of his players both on and off the court. Many of his former players still look at my dad as a father figure, and he will be the closest thing that they will ever have to a father this side of heaven. He has won over 600 games (and counting) in his illustrious, hall of fame coaching career, and he has impacted the lives of hundreds of young men.

However, if you were to ask my dad today if he has any regrets about coaching, he would likely end up in tears. My sister and I grew up watching a man often being more of a father to strangers than he was to his own children. My mom often saw a man that seemed more devoted to a leather ball and metal hoop than he was to her. My dad's win total soared while his church attendance fizzled. I spent my childhood observing a career consume my dad, and I vowed never to allow the same to happen to me.

Read the following two passages, and record what you learn from each regarding work.

1) **Psalm 127:1-2**

2) Ecclesiastes 4:7-8

Based on these passages, is it possible for believers to place too much importance on their work? Explain your answer.

Finally, let's spend a few minutes examining the importance of an often forgotten (but essential) component of work--rest. God created work, but He also created rest. We can't be at our best as workers unless we allow ourselves to occasionally take a break and recharge our batteries. Look up the following three passages, and note what you learn about rest below each.

1) Genesis 2:3

2) Exodus 20:8-11

3) Hebrews 4:1-11

In case you haven't learned it yet, our most most valuable resource in this world isn't money or our material possessions. It's time. As a physician, your time will be precious. You will have to learn the delicate balancing act of giving your patients and craft the time they deserve without neglecting the needs of your family, friends, and your commitments outside the walls of the hospital. Close this week in prayer, and ask God to help you learn how to better perform this difficult juggling act. Use the space below. Be specific, and ask God to rearrange your priorities as needed.

WEEK SEVEN

WITNESS WHILE YOU WORK, PART TWO

Day One

It was near the beginning of my junior year of college at the University of Kentucky when a random acquaintance asked me a question that would change the course of my life forever. I was standing at the water fountain, attempting to work out at our student fitness center when I heard a voice that I didn't recognize inquire from behind me: "Do you love Jesus?"

The question came from a guy named Daniel. I had randomly seen him in a few of my classes, and I had played "pick-up" basketball against him a couple of times, but we had never really spoken before. I found it quite interesting and perplexing that the first words he ever chose to speak to me were, "Do you love Jesus?" He didn't beat around the bush with small talk. He didn't waste his time on soup or salad--he went straight for the main course. It was a bold approach to talking to a stranger, and it definitely took me by surprise.

In retrospect, Daniel's question was clearly divine intervention. I grew up going to church, but during my first two years of college, my church attendance was sporadic at best. I was a "good kid" that knew right from wrong, but I didn't know Jesus. Daniel's random question changed that. The two of us became friends that day, and four years later, he stood beside me as the best man in my wedding. The impact on my life that stemmed from Daniel's simple question cannot be quantified by words, and I will be forever grateful for his boldness.

For so many Christians, their walk with Jesus starts with a conversation. For me, it was a conversation at the water fountain with Daniel. For others, it's a conversation with a neighbor or a co-worker. As a physician, you are constantly going to have the opportunity to interact with people (unless you are a radiologist and enjoy sitting alone in a dark room). You will be talking to patients, nurses, and staff on a daily basis, and you will have the chance to cultivate relationships with people who will trust every word you say and will constantly be looking to you for guidance.

Read the following passages, and note below each what you learn. More specifically, what do these verses speak to regarding your opportunity to impact the Kingdom at work?

1) **Romans 10:14-15**

2) Isaiah 6:8

3) Joshua 1:9

4) 2 Timothy 4:5

As a physician, you will have a golden opportunity to live out your faith at work. Don't squander it. Embrace it. As we learn about using our work as an opportunity to share the Gospel this week, I challenge you to be bold. Go out of your way to talk to one person about Jesus this week. You may feel uncomfortable at first, and that is perfectly OK. I remember feeling the same way. Just remember, a simple conversation about Jesus can go a long way--I'm living proof.

Day Two

"Preach the Gospel at all times, and when necessary, use words."
-Saint Francis of Assisi

I have always loved this quote. It serves as a reminder that our lives as believers are to be constant, living reflections of Jesus to the world around us. We are called to practice what we preach. When people interact with us on a regular basis, they should come away saying, "There is something different about that guy," even if we aren't boisterous Bible thumpers.

Our workplace is where we will spend the majority of our time outside of our home, and as physicians, it is a place where we will be under constant surveillance. Our workplace is where our patients will be observing our every move. It is where our nurses will be critiquing the way we practice medicine and the way we treat our patients. It is where our staff will be watching closely to see if we treat them as if they are invisible or a valued member of the team.

We can deal with this constant scrutiny in one of two ways. First, we can choose to be pompous and arrogant by reverting to the antiquated, paternalistic mindset that so many doctors have ingrained in their brains, and we can make sure that everyone knows that we are the most important person in the room. Second, we can humble ourselves and choose to be like Jesus.

Read **Matthew 23:12**, and look up the Greek word for humble. Record its definition below.

God's Word has much to say on humility, a concept foreign to most doctors. Look up the following passages and note what you learn from each.

1) **Philippians 2:3-4**

2)   **Ephesians 4:1-2**

3)   **1 Peter 5:6**

4)   **Proverbs 29:23**

5)   **Luke 14:7-11**

6)   **James 4:10**

7)   **Romans 11:18**

8) Proverbs 27:21

As a physician, you are going to have endless opportunities to preach the Gospel with your actions. In order to lead, we must first learn how to serve. Humble yourself, and take on the heart of a servant, just as Christ did. People around you will take notice.

Day Three

Throughout your residency, you will work alongside various "attending physicians." There are some that you will love to work with. There are others whose mere name will leave you feeling queasy. Some will serve as your mentors and role models, while others will make you ask yourself, "How on earth did that person get a medical degree?". You will take bits and pieces (both good and bad) from each of these teachers to mold the way you will practice medicine independently once you finish your training.

For me, there were a few physicians during residency that I would get excited about when I walked into the E.R. for a shift and saw them sitting in the captain's chair. The one that had the greatest impact on me was a guy named Dr. Jackson. Dr. Jackson was smart, easy-going, and great with patients. My wife told me that he was my "man crush," and I knew after working with him a couple of times that he was someone that I wanted to emulate. However, his biggest impact on me had nothing to do with the subtle nuances he taught me about diabetic ketoacidosis or intussusception in kids. While all of the wisdom he imparted to me about pediatric emergency medicine was important, it was the way that I watched him share his faith in the E.R. that will stick with me throughout the rest of my career. Until I met him, I had never seen a doctor openly discuss his faith with nurses, staff, and medical students. It was a beautiful and encouraging thing to behold. He was the only attending physician that I worked with throughout my residency that invited my family over to his home for dinner, and he served as a friend and mentor to me without even trying.

Look up the following five passages, and record what you learn from each one below. Pay careful attention to how each of these verses relates to how we can share the Gospel with our co-workers.

1) Titus 2:6-8

2) 1 Thessalonians 5:14-19

3) Colossians 4:2-6

4) 1 Thessalonians 2:7-8

5) Ezekiel 33:7-9

Outside of your family at home, your "work family" is the group of people that you will have the greatest chance to impact on a daily basis. Allow your faith to produce works through your work.

There are so many simple things we can do to "be Jesus" to those with whom we work. Here are a few examples that I came up with off the top my head:

1) Go out of your way to talk to your janitors and your clerical staff--they work very hard and often feel invisible and overlooked.

2) Learn everyone's name. Learn about their families. Genuinely have an interest in the lives of those you are working alongside.

3) Don't allow your staff to refer to you as "doctor." Every time a nurse refers to me as "Dr. Dodd," I always respond by calling them "Nurse ___" until they call me by my first name. We are all an integral part of the same team.

4) Get a patient a warm blanket or a cup of water instead of pawning it off on a nurse or a tech.

5) When you make a mess doing a procedure, clean it up yourself.

6) Buy lunch or breakfast for your staff every once in awhile. Pizza and donuts are not very expensive, but they are priceless to your nurses and staff.

This list clearly isn't exhaustive. There are dozens of other ways that we can humbly serve those we work alongside everyday that will display our faith. Selfless actions will lead to questions, and these questions will lead to conversations about Jesus. Use the space below to come up with a few ideas that you might have that will allow you to share the Gospel with your staff at work. Perhaps you will choose to take the bold approach like Daniel. Perhaps you would prefer to let your actions speak louder than your words like Saint Francis. Maybe you will be a Dr. Jackson to someone that looks up to you. No matter which path you choose, make your workplace your mission field.

Day Four

"What's the craziest thing you've ever seen in the E.R.?"

When I tell someone what I do for a living, this is the question that inevitably seems to follow. I already have a long list of crazy stories to choose from, and I have only been practicing emergency medicine for five and a half years. However, the cases that I remember most aren't usually the gorriest traumas or the ones in which I got lucky and "made a great save." My most memorable patients revolve around cases that evoke emotion.

Physicians are human beings with real emotions, and as a physician, you are going to encounter the full spectrum of human emotion. From the joy of a newborn baby's birth to the tragic and unexpected death of a loved one, you will be given a front row seat. You will be talking to patients and their family members at some of the most vulnerable moments in their lives. There is no easy way to tell someone that they have cancer or that their child has died, but you will have to do it.

It's unbelievable what patients will tell you as a physician. Complete strangers will grant you entrance into parts of their world to which no one else is given access. You will talk to people in some of their lowest moments, and they they will share with you some of the deepest and darkest recesses of their hearts. I remember during my third year of medical school, I was on my internal medicine rotation when I was sent into a patient's room to to get a history for a patient's annual well-check. I was having a good conversation with the elderly man that I had just met when he dropped a bombshell and told me, "Doc, I ain't got no balls." He went on to express to me that he was born with ambiguous genitalia, and his parents chose to make him a male. He had hidden this private secret from the attending that I was working with for decades (as well as from his new wife!), but for some reason that I will never understand, he trusted me, and he let me know that I was the first person he had ever told.

Your patients will literally entrust you with their lives. It's an incredible privilege and an enormous responsibility, but it's also a golden opportunity. Since most patients take what their doctors say as gospel, it seems to reason that we should show them the Gospel.

Read the following four passages, and note what you learn below each. How do these verses apply to sharing the Gospel with your patients?

1) **1 Peter 3:15-17**

2) Mark 2:15-17

3) James 2:1-9

4) Luke 12:8-9

Not all patients are going to be receptive of the Gospel, but that shouldn't stop us from looking for opportunities to do it. If a patient is wearing a church T-shirt or a cross necklace, it is OK to ask them about it. If you see a tattoo that relates to the Bible, inquire about it. If you have just broken bad news to a patient or their family, it's OK to offer to pray with them. If you are performing a long laceration repair, don't just sit there in silence, but "make the most of every opportunity" **(Ephesians 5:16)**.

The ways that you share the Gospel with your patients will obviously differ depending on your specialty and your practice setting, but don't miss out on opportunities to make an impact on your patients lives. Use the space on the following page to think of some practical ways that you can share the Gospel with your patients. Be creative. Remember--physical healing is temporary, but spiritual healing is eternal.

Day Five

Medicine seems pretty straight-forward during your first two years of medical school. A patient presents with X symptoms. You give them a Y diagnosis. You fix them with Z treatment. Done and done. On to the next case.

Unfortunately, you quickly learn during your third year of medical school that patients don't read the same textbooks that you did, and in the real world, "textbook cases" are more rare than unicorns. You also quickly learn that obtaining a good history from some patients is like pulling teeth and that talking to others is about as pleasant an experience as listening to your children scream from the backseat during a long road trip. This is why some of you may become radiologists.

The difficult patient is centerstage in the E.R., and I have had the pleasure of witnessing numerous virtuoso performances. Over the past few years, I have been cursed at, spit on, and yelled at by some of the most self-destructive and decrepit pieces of protoplasm that walk the earth. Like dementors, these needy people seem to suck the life right out of you, but underneath their angry facade, there often lies a lost soul longing for Jesus. We must never lose sight of that fact. We must take the higher road. Like Jesus, we must learn to love the unlovable.

Read the following passages, and record what you learn from each one. How do these verses relate to the way we are called to treat those that the world turns its back on? How do the words of these verses pertain to loving the unlovable, especially in the realm of medicine?

1) 2 Timothy 2:24-26

2) Matthew 5:38-48

3) Matthew 18:21-22

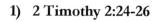

4) Luke 6:27-36

5) Hebrews 12:1-3

These verses don't just apply to difficult patients. Throughout the course of your career, you will undoubtedly be working alongside colleagues, nurses, and other providers that may not be the easiest people in the world to work with. Not everyone you work with will share your Christian beliefs, and some may even despise you for your faith. Personality clashes may be inevitable, but it is the way that you handle difficult situations with difficult people that will be the true testament of your faith to those around you. When you find yourself in such precarious circumstances, seek after God, and with His help, you will do mighty things (**Psalm 108:13**).

I pray that these past two weeks have been fruitful for you and that you now have a much clearer and more complete understanding of work from a biblical perspective. Spend the next few minutes using the space below to summarize the main things that God has taught you about work over the past two weeks. Be specific. How has He changed your heart?

Let's close this week in prayer:

"Lord, thank You for the privilege of work. Help us to embrace our work with a joyful attitude, and allow us to seek out chances at work to impact those around us. Teach us to preach the Gospel with our actions, and help us to be a light for You no matter the circumstances. Father, never allow me to waste an opportunity. Amen."

WEEK EIGHT

MARRIAGE: MADE IN HEAVEN

Day One

"The man who finds a wife finds a treasure, and he receives favor from the LORD."
-Proverbs 18:22 (NLT)

When my wife and I moved to Charleston, South Carolina for residency, we bought a two-person, yellow kayak from Craigslist. Before we had our first child, we would frequently take it out and paddle around the the inlets of the lowcountry. It was a wonderful way for us to enjoy God's creation while spending time alone together. We would frequently get within a few feet of dolphins, we would have great conversations, and it was typically a very enjoyable and relaxing experience. One day, we decided to paddle all the way out to Fort Sumter to see the historical Civil War site. The paddle out was easy--it took us about forty minutes. However, the paddle back was a different story. I failed to consider the direction of the tide when I planned our voyage, and the return trip home took nearly three hours. Amanda was beyond frustrated when we were paddling as hard as humanly possible, yet somehow, our kayak was moving backwards. The last hour was miserable. I couldn't feel my arms. Amanda was giving me the silent treatment. Our relaxing date had turned into an exhausting debacle. When we got home, we were both tired and frustrated. As we carried the kayak from the car to our back porch, Amanda reminded me that we had never given our kayak a name, so we christened it "The Marriage Builder." We sold the kayak when we moved back to Kentucky, but hopefully, its new owners find it to be as edifying as we did.

Marriage isn't always easy, but it is the most sacred and highly esteemed relationship that God has given us with another human being. It is challenging yet fulfilling. It is difficult yet rewarding. It is a beautifully complicated mystery that requires continual work from both parties.

This week, we are going to dive into God's Word and learn what it tells us regarding the subject of marriage. Perhaps you are already married. Maybe you are engaged or single. No matter your relationship status, I pray that this week's study will be fruitful.

We can't fully understand marriage unless we first go back to its roots. God established marriage in Genesis, and we will revisit this important book each day throughout the week. Read the following two passages, record what you learn from each, and then answer the questions that follow.

1) Genesis 1:26-31

2) Genesis 2:20-25

Who established marriage?

What was Adam's response to God creating woman? Was he disappointed? Was he excited? Explain your answer.

What were Adam and Eve's initial responses to one another?

Now that we know the origins of marriage, let's fast forward to the New Testament and dissect one of the most significant passages in all of scripture when it comes to marriage. These verses are engraved on the inside of my wedding band and serve as the foundation for the intimate relationship between my wife and myself. You have likely heard or read these words before, but don't allow them to feel familiar. Read them as if they are brand new to you.

Ephesians 5:22-33 (ESV)

Wives, submit to your own husbands, as to the Lord. For the husband is the head of the wife even as Christ is the head of the church, his body, and is himself its Savior. Now as the church submits to Christ, so also wives should submit in everything to their husbands.

Husbands, love your wives, as Christ loved the church and gave himself up for her, that he might sanctify her, having cleansed her by the washing of water with the word, so that he might present the church to himself in splendor, without spot or wrinkle or any such thing, that she might be holy and without blemish. In the same way husbands should love their wives as their own bodies. He who loves his wife loves himself. For no one ever hated his own flesh, but nourishes and cherishes it, just as Christ does the church, because we are members of his body. "Therefore a man shall leave his father and mother and hold fast to his wife, and the two shall become one flesh." This mystery is profound, and I am saying that it refers to Christ and the church. However, let each one of you love his wife as himself, and let the wife see that she respects her husband.

Read through these verses several times. Use the space below to list the God-given roles and purposes of both the husband and the wife. Be thorough, and pay attention to details.

Look up the Greek definitions for the following words, and record their definitions below.

1) Submit (v. 24)

2) Love (v. 25)

3) Gave (v. 25)

4) Hold Fast (v. 31)

If you are married, how would you rate your performance as a spouse based solely on this passage? What could you improve on? Be honest. If you are single, what parts of this passage seem to be particularly challenging?

Day Two

I don't know if you are aware, but there is an ongoing war taking place in America today. It's not a war against ISIS. It's not a war against racism. It's a war on manhood. Our politically correct society (in which everyone gets a trophy and uses the same bathroom) has replaced the strong and courageous warrior of God with the weak and timid wimp. Masculine leaders have gone the way of the dodo bird, and men are no longer the pursuers but are now the pursued. Men have become emasculated, and with current cultural trends, this phenomenon doesn't seem to be turning around anytime soon.

When you close your eyes and envision the model of the biblical man, what do you see? What does he look like? What characteristics does he display? How does your man stack up against society's modern man?

Now that you have your pre-conceived picture of what a Godly man should look like, let's examine what the Bible tells us about the role of a man. As we established two weeks ago, God made man to be a leader, a provider, and a worker. Again, read **Genesis 2:20-25**, and answer the questions that follow.

Based on this passage, what was woman's original role? What was man's?

Now read **Genesis 3**, and answer the following questions.

Who did the serpent appeal to first, Adam or Eve? Why do you think he chose this person rather than the other?

Where was Adam when Eve chose to sin? What was the immediate result of his disobedience?

Who did Adam blame for what happened?

How did God punish Adam for his sin? What were the consequences for men of future generations as a result of his lack of leadership?

As you can see, leadership is something that man has struggled with from the very beginning. However, it doesn't have to be that way for us today because through His Word, God has given us a blueprint for biblical manhood. Men still have a chance to redeem themselves. Read the following verses and note what you learn about the role of a man.

1) **Colossians 3:19**

2) 1 Peter 3:7

3) 1 Corinthians 11:3

4) 1 Timothy 5:8

Finally, let's examine **1 Timothy 3**. In this passage, Paul lays out the qualifications of elders and deacons. While not all men are called to these church offices, there is much that we can learn about what an honorable and righteous man of God looks like by closely examining these verses. Use the space below to record the characteristics and requirements of God's "model man." Does this description resemble you? Do you see any areas for improvement in your life?

Day Three

If you think men have it rough today, try walking in a woman's shoes. The beautiful and fulfilling job of being a wife and mother is now looked down upon by our society as archaic and sexist. Women are portrayed in popular culture as nothing more than sex objects. Christian female role models are few and far between, and the desire to be a wife and mother while allowing the husband to "wear the pants" in the family has been replaced by the desire for a career and women wearing pantsuits.

Let's repeat our exercise from yesterday. When you close your eyes and envision the model of the biblical woman, what do you see? What does she look like? What characteristics does she exhibit? How does your woman compare to society's modern woman?

Again, let's return to the book of Genesis. Reread **Genesis 3**, and answer the following questions.

Who do you feel sinned first, Adam or Eve? Why do you feel that way?

How did Eve respond when God asked her what had happened?

What were the long-term consequences for women of future generations because of the fall?

Unfortunately, today's culture has misconstrued the biblical woman into a wife that never leaves the kitchen, is forbidden to open her mouth, and does exactly as she is told. God's Word paints a different picture. Read the following passages and record what you learn from each about the role of a wife.

1) **1 Corinthians 11:11-12**

2) **Colossians 3:18**

3) **Titus 2:3-5**

4) 1 Peter 3:1-6

5) 1 Timothy 2:9-15

6) Proverbs 12:4

7) Proverbs 19:14

8) Proverbs 21:9 and 19, Proverbs 27:15, Proverbs 25:24

Finally, let's take a close look at **Proverbs 31**. This passage is classically referred to as the blueprint for God's "model woman." As you read these verses, take note of the characteristics displayed by a biblical woman. If you are a woman, how do you compare? If you are a married man, does this woman resemble your wife? How can you help your wife become more like her? If you are single, does this passage change the qualities that you should be looking for in a potential spouse?

Day Four

Now that you have a more in depth understanding of the biblical roles of man and woman in the marriage relationship, let's tackle one of the most important issues that plagues so many marriages today. Sex. This week just got more interesting, didn't it?

We know what the world tells us about sex. Sex is everywhere we look. Sex outside of marriage is rampant. Fornication and adultery are often cheered for and celebrated in movies and television. America is in the midst of a pornography epidemic that has cheapened and perverted one of God's most beautiful gifts into a few fleeting moments of pleasure with the simple click of a mouse. But what does God's Word tell us about sex?

Again, let's return to the book of Genesis. Reread **Genesis 1:27-28**. What does God command Adam and Eve to do in verse 28? This isn't a trick question.

Reread Genesis **2:22-25**. What do you think God means in verse 24 when He says, "they shall become one flesh?" What were Adam and Eve's attitude toward nakedness and sex in verse 25?

Now fast forward to the the fall of man, and read **Genesis 3:7**. How does the knowledge of sin affect Adam and Eve?

After studying through the first three chapters of Genesis, who created and designed sex? Was sex a result of the fall, or was it created by God before the fall? Why do you feel that way?

Sex was created and ordained by God to be the most intimate relationship we have with another human being. It is an exclusive gift meant to be shared between one husband and one wife. It was designed for procreation but also for enjoyment and pleasure. It is somehow a physical and emotional act at the same time. It is something that we crave, and when done right, it is one of the most beautifully satisfying and selfless acts that one could ever imagine. Read the following two passages, and note what you learn from each about sex.

1) **1 Corinthians 7:1-5**

2) **Proverbs 5:18-19**

Sex within marriage is a subject so near and dear to God's heart that he devoted an entire book of the Bible to it. **Song of Solomon** is an Old Testament book that you probably never read in Sunday school. In fact, it is said that Jewish men were not allowed to read this book until they had reached adulthood. You will soon understand why. Finish today by reading **Song of Solomon**. It's only eight short chapters, and I promise that its contents will keep you captivated. It can be a bit difficult to follow at first, so use the following outline to keep you on track as you read:

1. The Courtship (**1-3:5**)
2. The Wedding (**3:6-11**)
3. The Wedding Night (**4:1-5:1**)
4. The Maturation of Marriage (**5:2-8:14**)

There are so many important insights to glean from this book about dating, marriage, and sex. As you read, take note of how the bride and groom communicate both verbally and physically before they are married, after they are married, and in the bedroom on their wedding night. Record all that you learn below.

Day Five

Divorce. It's an ugly word that we are all unfortunately far too familiar with, and its deep scars leave broken families and bitter hearts in its wake. A large percentage of the marriages in our country end in divorce, and physicians are not immune. The vast majority of divorces in America center around money, infidelity, or a feeling of neglect from one spouse. Doctors are compensated well, work long hours, and they often work alongside young, attractive, and impressionable nurses. It's a perfect storm of vulnerability, and unless our marriages are rooted in the Word, they are susceptible to crumbling.

When God created the institution of marriage, He designed it to be permanent. Once again, read **Genesis 2:24**. What do you think God meant in this verse? Why do you feel that way?

This verse was clearly near and dear to Jesus' heart as well. Flip over to the New Testament and read **Matthew 19:1-12**. What do you learn from Jesus' response to the Pharisees? Examine verse **8** carefully. What was God's original intention for marriage?

Let's take a close look at some other important passages that explore both the sanctity of marriage and God's perspective on divorce. As you read each, note what you learn.

1) **Malachi 2:13-16 (NASB)**

2) **Matthew 5:27-32**

3) **Mark 10:1-12**

4) **Luke 16:18**

5) **Romans 7:2-3**

6) **1 Corinthians 7:10-16**

7) **Hebrews 13:4**

Based on all that you have studied today, how do you now feel about divorce? Has scripture changed your opinion on the permanence of marriage? Is divorce biblical? Is it of God, or was it created by man? Use the space below to express your thoughts.

Your crash course on biblical marriage is now complete. Clearly, a five day study on marriage is not comprehensive, but hopefully, you now have a more complete understanding of what God intended marriage to be. If you are married, how has this week changed your perspective on marriage? How will your marriage look different going forward based on the biblical truths that you have learned?

If you are single, consider yourself fortunate that you now have a greater understanding of biblical marriage than do many men in our country that are already married. Don't let this wisdom go to waste. If you are called to be single, God bless you--you are a stronger man than I am. If you desire to be married one day, how will the insights you learned this week affect your pursuit of a future spouse?

Let's close this week in prayer:

"Lord, we thank You for the incredible gift of marriage. Help us to love sacrificially. Allow us to fully grasp what it means to love our wives as Christ loved the church. Help us to embrace our roles as husbands and wives with open arms. Let two become one, and let no man separate the sanctity of what You have designed. Amen."

WEEK NINE

RAISING KIDS GOD'S WAY

Day One

"Behold, children are a heritage from the Lord, the fruit of the womb a reward. Like arrows in the hand of a warrior are the children of one's youth. Blessed is the man who fills his quiver with them! He shall not be put to shame when he speaks with his enemies in the gate."
--Psalm 127:3-5 (ESV)

January 5, 2013 is a day that I will never forget. It's the day that I became a father. It's the day that God blessed me with an incredible gift-- a baby girl named Lucy. We chose her name because it meant "bringer of light," and she has brightened my world in a way that I never could have imagined. Friends had told me that I wouldn't be able to understand the unspeakable joy of becoming a father until I actually experienced it myself, and they were one hundred percent correct. Two years later, God blessed me with a son, and Lord willing, our third little bundle of joy (Annie) will be born this summer. Clearly, I didn't subscribe to the "a boy for me, a girl for you, and now we're through" school of thought. I took **Psalm 127:3-5** to heart--my quiver is getting heavy.

Children are one of God's most precious gifts. He has bestowed on us the awesome responsibility for another human life. He has given us blank canvases to paint and unformed lumps of clay to mold. Some parents embrace this opportunity with open arms and diligently work for years at creating a masterpiece for God to enjoy for eternity while others lazily go through the motions of parenthood and let the paint go to waste and watch the clay dry out.

This week, we are going to explore what God's Word has to tell us about parenting. If you are already a parent, I pray that the insights you glean over the coming days will help guide you in raising Godly children that come to know and love the Lord. If you are single, and children aren't yet even on your radar, I pray that you will store up what you learn in your heart so that it overflows into your children when the time is right for you to become a parent.

As I'm sure you have probably figured out already, I love kids. And for some reason unbeknownst to me, kids have always seemed to love me, too. Maybe I should have been a pediatrician. However, the enormous heart that God has given me toward children pales in comparison to His. Children are special to God. He has a heart for children that is unmatched by any earthly relationship, and my unconditional love for my own children will always fall short of His eternal love for them.

Read the following passages, and record your insights below. As you read these verses, pay special attention to God's attitude toward children.

1) Jeremiah 1:4-8

2) Psalm 139:13-16

3) Matthew 19:13-14

4) Mark 9:42

5) 1 Timothy 4:12

6) Amos 1:13-14

Based on these passages, when does God's relationship with children begin? How does He view children?

After reading these verses, what did you learn about your responsibility to children as a role model, teacher, and/or parent?

Day Two

Did you know any doctor's kids growing up? What were they like? What kind of relationship did they have with their physician parent? If your experience is anything like mine, so many of these kids unfortunately had absent parents because mom or dad was so busy practicing as a physician that they neglected their primary responsibilities to their spouse and or/children. I don't want your kids to have that experience.

Today, we are going to observe several parental examples from the Old Testament, but rather than presenting you with glowing, biblical examples of model fathers, I am going to do the opposite. We are going to do some case studies on some famous biblical fathers and explore where they fell short as dads. As you read through each of the following passages, think about the consequences of the actions (or inactions) of each of these fathers. Record your insights, and then answer the questions that follow.

1) Isaac: Genesis 25:20-28 and Genesis 27:1-41

2) Jacob (son of Isaac): Genesis 37:3-35

3) Lot: Genesis 19:1-8 and 19:30-36

4) Eli: 1 Samuel 2:12-17, 22-25

5) Samuel ("adopted" son of Eli): 1 Samuel 8:1-3

6) David: 2 Samuel 11:2-17 and 1 Chronicles 3:1-5

7) Solomon (son of David): 1 Kings 11:1-10

Are there any apparent consequences to playing favorites among children?

Did you notice any patterns or trends between the sins of certain fathers and their sons? Does sin appear to be a learned habit?

Some of these men did some truly heinous things. They were murderers, adulterers, and rapists. They were so busy fulfilling their other earthly roles and seeking after their own fleshly desires that they were often absent, lousy fathers. Yet, David was the linchpin in the lineage of Jesus and a "man after God's own heart" (**Acts 13:22**). God considered Lot righteous (**2 Peter 2:7**), and Isaac, Jacob, and Samuel are all mentioned in the "Heroes of the Faith Hall of Fame" in **Hebrews 11**. Can you imagine how much more impactful these famous men could have been for God's Kingdom had they been better fathers?

Not all fathers in the Bible were horrendous examples. Let's quickly fast forward to the New Testament. In **Acts 6:5**, we are introduced to Philip the Evangelist. He is one of the seven original apostles (chosen by Jesus' disciples) that were appointed with the momentous task of leading the early Christian church. Throughout **Acts 8**, we watch Philip perform miracles, preach the Gospel with boldness, and baptize new believers. At the end of the chapter, he becomes the only man in human history to experience teleportation via the Holy Spirit! Philip clearly is a man of importance to God, and he appears to be on a fast path to fame within the early church as one of its most prominent leaders. However, after being teleported in Acts **8:39-40** (read these verses--I dare you not to be amazed!), Philip subsequently disappears for the next twenty years, and we don't see him resurface again until **Acts 21**. Read **Acts 21:8-9**, and note what you learn about Philip's current situation in Caesarea.

What can we infer from these passages regarding what Philip has been doing for the past twenty years? What do we learn about Philip as a father and about his example to his daughters? What does Philip's story teach us about humility and about establishing a household?

Fortunately, we have a Father in heaven that is a far greater example to us than are any of these earthly men. He loves us so unconditionally despite our innumerable flaws that He sacrificed His only Son on our behalf. Spend a few minutes in prayer and thank Him for being such a good, good Father to you. Finally, use the space below to write down a few of the insights you learned today about "what not to do" as a parent. Learn from the mistakes of others so that you won't make them yourself.

Days Three and Four

As we discussed a few weeks ago, a physician's greatest resource is their time, and nowhere is this more evident than when you first become a parent. Parenthood forces you to instantly learn that your life is no longer your own. You will take your baby home from the hospital and come to the sudden realization that you and your spouse are fully responsible for the life of another human being. Did you just develop palpitations?

The God-given responsibility of raising children can sometimes feel overwhelming, but just like generations of parents have done for centuries before us, we learn the ropes as we go. You can read every expert parenting book written in human history before having your first child, but there is no way to simulate the experience of being a mom or dad until you are in the trenches. Luckily, as believers, we don't have to wing it--we have the Bible as our guide to help us along the way. Read each of the following passages and record below each what you learn regarding your role as a parent.

1) **Exodus 20:12**

2) **Deuteronomy 6:4-9**

3) **Ephesians 6:1-4**

4) **2 Timothy 3:14-17**

5) **Psalm 40:8**

6) Colossians 3:20-21

7) Deuteronomy 5:16

8) Luke 6:40

9) 1 Corinthians 15:33

10) Psalm 1:1-2

11) Psalm 78:1-8

God's Word makes it quite clear that we are called to fully invest in the lives of our children. We are given a finite window of time to raise our children at home. Our culture in America gives us eighteen years to prepare our children for eternity, and as I'm already beginning to learn, those eighteen years will fly by. I don't want to squander my opportunity. I don't want to stand idly by and pawn off my responsibility of raising Godly children on a "youth group" leader or a Sunday school teacher that sees my child once a week while I watch from the sidelines. I want to be in the game!

It is mine and Amanda's God-given duty as parents to bring up our children in the "discipline and instruction of the Lord" (**Ephesians 6:4**). Living out this verse will look very different for different families--allow me to give you a glimpse into ours.

In our home, we have attempted to start a daily "family worship time" that consists of singing, praying, and reading from the Bible together. My random work schedule can make this endeavor challenging, and some days are more successful than others, but we are trying to consistently incorporate worshipping the Lord together into our daily lives so that it becomes second nature for our children. I don't just want to tell my children what it means to follow Jesus every day. I want to personify **1 John 3:18** and show them what it means to live out the Gospel. I want to disciple them. Right now, my wife and I both feel that the best way to disciple our children during their most malleable years is by homeschooling them. Your palpitations just came back, didn't they? I know what you are thinking right now. Homeschool kids are weird. Homeschool kids are too sheltered. Homeschool kids are social misfits. Homeschool kids can't play sports. Ten years ago, I would have said all the same things, but then I read a book written by Voddie Baucham entitled *Family Driven Faith* that forced me to do a 180 degree turn on my original position. Dr. Baucham is a world-renowned author, speaker, and pastor, but he is first and foremost a husband and a father. His book completely changed my attitude toward homeschooling and helped me to fully understand its utility in discipling my children. My wife and I believe that if it is our primary responsibility as parents to disciple our children, we can't justify sending them to school for more than forty hours a week for more than nine months a year for thirteen years of their short childhood to be discipled by a complete stranger that may or may not share our biblical worldview and faith. Dr. Baucham challenged me to embrace my biblical responsibility as a leader and a father, and he revealed the importance of establishing multi-generational faithfulness within my own family. His words of wisdom allowed me to grasp an incredibly important concept that I had never really considered before reading his book--the way that I raise my children will impact the way that they raise their children and so on and so forth for generations to come. It's a great book, and I would highly recommend it to any young father that is striving to lead his family toward heaven.

Let's get practical. Based on what you have learned over the past two days, take a few minutes and write down some of the truths the Lord has revealed to you. What verses stood out to you most? How do you plan on living out **Ephesians 6:4** and **Deuteronomy 6:4-9**? If you are already a parent, do you currently make worshipping the Lord together as a family a priority? Are you discipling your children on a daily basis? What are some ways in which you could improve as a parent? If you are not yet a parent, what did you learn that might help better prepare you for parenthood? What facets of parenting do you think will present you with the biggest challenges?

Day Five

Let's close this week by revisiting Solomon's words of wisdom regarding raising Godly children by turning our eyes to the book of Proverbs. As you read each of the following verses, think about how each one could help you improve as a parent, and then answer the questions that follow.

1) Proverbs 22:6

2) Proverbs 30:17

3) Proverbs 1:8-9

4) Proverbs 20:7

5) Proverbs 28:7

6) Proverbs 29:15-17

7) **Proverbs 13:24**

8) **Proverbs 22:15**

9) **Proverbs 23:13-14**

10) **Proverbs 23:24-25**

After reading these verses, did you learn anything new about disciplining your children?

What did you learn about the importance of establishing a biblical foundation in a child at a young age?

How will the way you choose to disciple your children affect your family's future generations?

Let's close our week in prayer:

"Lord, we thank You for the precious gift of children. We thank You for the beautiful responsibility that You have entrusted us with as parents, and we embrace the opportunity of raising a child in the discipline and instruction of the Lord. Give us wisdom, and give us patience. Allow us to disciple our children in a way that will impact generations to come. Help us to teach our children to love You and live for You in a way that will make heaven a more crowded place to live for eternity. Amen."

WEEK TEN

GIVING BACK

Day One

I know it's hard to believe, but we have reached the last week of our study. Thank you so much for your faithfulness and for investing your precious time into God's Word. Your labor has not been in vain. I pray that your diligence has been fruitful and that the biblical truths you have learned over the past several weeks will have eternal consequences for both you and those that you will impact throughout your career as a physician.

We are going to spend this last week exploring what God's Word teaches us about "giving back." In a few short years, you will finish your training, graduate from residency, and step out into the world as a shiny, new "attending physician." At first, your patients will probably tell you that you don't look old enough to be a doctor, and you will spend your first few weeks after residency growing a beard to look more mature while adjusting to practicing medicine on your own for the first time. Next, you will open up your first "real" paycheck, and you will immediately pinch yourself to make sure you aren't dreaming. You will then come to the sudden realization that you now have the means to "do stuff," and that "stuff" will be the focus of our study this week.

However, before we begin diving headfirst into what "giving back" entails, I would be amiss if we didn't first devote a day of study to the important subject of prayer. Prayer is a central component of the Christian faith and an essential element in learning to give biblically. It is both a commandment and a gift from our Heavenly Father that allows us to communicate with the same God that created the world we live in. It gives us the ability as believers to intercede on behalf of others so that they may experience God in a way they may never have previously imagined. The power of prayer cannot be understated.

Biblical experts have written countless books on the topic of prayer, so today clearly isn't meant to be a comprehensive study on the subject. However, studying through the following verses should help you to grasp the importance of prayer in the life of a believer and better understand its purpose. Read the following passages, record what you learn below each, and then answer the questions that follow.

1) James 5:16

2) Philippians 4:6-7

3) Mark 11:24-25

4) Matthew 21:22

5) 1 Thessalonians 5:16-18

6) Ephesians 6:16-18

7) Jeremiah 33:2-3

8) Matthew 6:5-15

9) 1 Timothy 2:1-4

10) Ephesians 3:14-21

Based on these passages, for what and for whom are we called to pray?

When should we pray?

What is the result of a righteous man's prayer?

What is your prayer life currently like? How could it improve?

Close today in prayer. Thank God for giving you this incredible gift that we all too often take for granted, and ask Him to reveal to you this week what giving back truly means.

Days Two and Three

As we learned a few weeks ago from **Luke 12:48**, "to whom much is given, much will be required." You may not have realized it at the time, but Dr. Luke was talking directly to you. Physicians are compensated very well for their services, and the way that we distribute the money that we have been blessed with should be a direct reflection of God's blessing to us.

Let's quickly revisit two passages to refresh our memories in regards to the origin of our bank accounts. Reread **Psalm 24:1** and **1 Chronicles 29:13-16**, and note what you learn below.

The money that God has entrusted us with ultimately belongs to Him. However, He has given us the ability to choose what to do with it. We can either give Him back a portion of what He has given us, or we can choose to keep it all for ourselves. For example, I know a doctor that upon completing residency threw a massive "waste my first paycheck party." I'm going to go out on a limb and say that this probably wasn't the best way to honor God with his newfound wealth. Over the next two days, we are going to examine the Word for insight into how God calls us to "give back" financially.

Tithing is a concept that most Christians are familiar with. When I was a kid, I thought "tithing" simply meant throwing a few dollars into a silver plate that got passed around during the church service. It turns out I was wrong. The origins of tithing go back several thousand years. Its first mention is in Genesis **14:18-20**. Read this passage, and record what you learn below. Additionally, look up the Hebrew transliteration for the word "tithe" and record its definition.

The next mention of tithing comes from Abraham's grandson, Jacob, in **Genesis 28:20-22**. Read this passage, and note what you learn.

Based on these two passages, was tithing originally a requirement from God or a free will offering to God from Abraham and Jacob? Why do you feel that way?

Several hundred years later, things changed when God established the Old Covenant through Moses. He introduced tithing as a commandment as part of the Old Law. Read **Leviticus 27:30-32** and **Numbers 18:21-24**, and note what you learn. Pay special attention to the purpose of Israel's tithes in regards to the Levites.

In addition to the Levitical tithe, Israelites were commanded to give two other tithes as well. The Festival Tithe (**Deuteronomy 26:10-16**) was an annual tithe used to fund a yearly festival called the Feast of Tabernacles, and the Charity Tithe (**Deuteronomy 14:28-29**) was given twice every seven years to help support sojourners, orphans, widows, and provide additional resources for the Levites. Do the math. The average Israelite was commanded to donate approximately 23% of their earnings every year in tithes alone!

Finally, read **Malachi 3:8-10**, and note what you learn about God's attitude toward tithing.

Tithing clearly was an essential part of the Old Law. It was a commandment from God that served a clear purpose. However, when Jesus established the New Covenant through his sacrificial death and resurrection, tithing became a little less clearcut. While the New Testament doesn't present us with an exact percentage of how much money we are called to give back to God, it tells us a great deal about how we are called to give. Read the following passages, note what you learn from each, and then answer the questions that follow.

1) **Proverbs 3:9**

2) **Matthew 6:1-4**

3) 1 John 3:16-18

4) 2 Corinthians 8:1-15

5) Galatians 6:10

6) Romans 12:13

7) Mark 12:41-44

8) Luke 18:9-14

9) 2 Corinthians 9:6-11

10) 1 Timothy 6:17-19

Based on these passages, what should our attitude be toward giving/tithing?

What does God's Word tell us about giving sacrificially?

What are some of the purposes of tithing? To what causes should our money go?

While the New Testament may not tell us that we are required to give a specific percentage of our income in the form of a "tithe," it does give us very specific commandments as to how we are called to give sacrificially, generously, willingly, and cheerfully. We are to give God our first fruits. So how much should we give? That is a decision that must be made prayerfully between you and God. In my humble opinion, you should give as much as you possibly can--it's God's money anyway. As physicians, rather than increasing our standard of living, perhaps we should increase our standard of giving. As a matter of fact, maybe we are asking the wrong question when we ask, "How much should we give?" Instead, perhaps we should be asking ourselves, "How much should we keep?"

Day Four

"Christians are like manure: spread them out and they help everything grow better, but keep them in one big pile and they stink horribly."

--Francis Chan

The summer before I started medical school, I chose to go on a medical mission trip to Mexico City. For two weeks, I was part of a group of Americans that helped serve some of Mexico City's most forgotten people. It was an experience that I will never forget. I never truly realized how fortunate I was until I saw with my own two eyes what real poverty looked like. One day, we visited one of the city's largest garbage dumps on the outskirts of town. I soon came to learn that this massive heap of trash with an indescribable stench served as the home of dozens of Mexican families. I was awestruck. The only thing more shocking to me than the smell were the attitudes of the people that I met there. Every child that I saw had a smile on their face. It's as if they didn't even realize that they were poor. These impoverished people that I initially considered to be incredibly unfortunate were literally rummaging through garbage to survive. Yet, not a single person that I encountered complained about their circumstances, and they were all genuinely appreciative of our visit in a way that words can't adequately explain. Needless to say, it was quite a humbling experience, and that day made **Deuteronomy 4:9** come to life for me.

As a physician, God has blessed you with both the financial means and the unique skill set to impact not only the community that you live in but also others around the globe. We shouldn't neglect this blessing. Read the following passages, and note what you learn below.

1) **Matthew 28:19-20**

2) **Acts 1:8**

3) Acts 13:47

4) Mark 16:15

5) Mark 13:10

6) Matthew 24:14

7) Romans 10:14-15

As we learned a few weeks ago, we are called as believers to exemplify the Gospel to our families, our neighbors, our patients, our co-workers, and the people in our communities that we interact with on a daily basis. However, we are also commanded by God to take Jesus to "the ends of the earth." As a doctor, you have a built-in avenue to reach unreached people. Medicine is a powerful tool. Use it. The beauty of representing Jesus to the sick that live abroad is something we can't fully experience in our American bubble. I believe the only way to practice medicine as a Christian physician in its purest form is as a medical missionary. There is no insurance. There is no fear of litigation. There is no electronic medical record. There is simply a sick patient, and a doctor that wants to help them feel better. While you may have a limited armamentarium of medical interventions to choose from in these resource scarce portions of the world, you will be armed with the unlimited power of the Gospel in a way that you would never be granted access to in an American hospital or clinic. You will be able to display the heart of Jesus in an uninhibited way, and you will quickly recognize that there is no language barrier big enough to keep out the Holy Spirit.

If you have a big heart for international medicine, perhaps you should consider an international medicine fellowship. My buddy Joel did just that, and he has already been blessed with the opportunity to be the hands and feet of Jesus to people in need in the Caribbean, South America, Africa, and Asia. I hope to start going on international medical mission trips regularly with him in the coming years. I want to bring along my wife and my children so that our family can fulfill the Great Commision together. I want them to experience **Deuteronomy 4:9** for themselves the same way that I did in Mexico City. Our memories may last for a lifetime, but our impact will last for eternity.

Day Five

"Before the judgment seat of Christ, my service will be judged not by how much I have done, but by how much I could have done."

                                            --A.W. Tozer

As we close our study, I would like to leave you with a benediction and some final words of encouragement.

When you really think about it, doctors are a little bit crazy. What other group of people puts themselves into hundreds of thousands of dollars of debt to spend some of the best years of their lives with their noses stuck in books and the goal of working for minimum wage for several years after obtaining a prestigious, professional degree? Once they finish their training, they work long hours that will leave them both physically and emotionally drained, and the difficult patients that they will undoubtedly take care of throughout their careers will often leave them jaded toward society. What sane person would sign up for that job description?

We have a tough job. I have met several doctors that have told me that if they had the ability to go back in time, they would have chosen another profession. I pray that you will not be one of those doctors. I can honestly tell you that I can't think of any other job that I would rather do (although professional golf does look pretty tempting). Some patients may be difficult and some days might be challenging, but I have the opportunity to impact lives in a way that very few people get to experience. My job is incredibly rewarding. The pros far outweigh the cons, and in the end, all of the hard work and sacrifice is worth the privilege of being a doctor to the world.

Don't allow yourself to become jaded. Change the culture around you. Pray continually, and learn to love the Word. Invest in the lives of your families, your coworkers, and your patients. Look for opportunities to serve. Use your time, your talents, and your treasures for God's glory. Embrace the gifts of marriage and children, and train up the next generation to be warriors for the Lord. Make disciples, make sacrifices, and give back as much as you can. Be Jesus to those around you, and imitate The Great Physician.

Look up the following verses and note what you learn from each.

1) **Matthew 7:24-27**

2) **John 14:15**

3) **John 14:23**

You have studied through hundreds of verses over the past several weeks, so you have clearly heard the Word. Now it's time to put them into practice. How will you use what you have learned to follow His commandments, and what will be the end result of your faithfulness?

Use the rest of today to summarize what stood out most to you from God's Word over the past ten weeks. Take as much time as you need. May God bless you for your faithfulness and may "the grace of the Lord Jesus Christ and the love of God and the fellowship of the Holy Spirit be with you all" (**2 Corinthians 13:14**).

THE GOSPEL IN A NUTSHELL

"The Gospel is the news that Jesus Christ, the Righteous One, died for our sins and rose again, eternally triumphant over all his enemies, so that there is now no condemnation for those who believe, but only everlasting joy."

--John Piper

The Greek word for "gospel" literally translates "good news"--I can't think of another word with a more perfect definition. The Gospel is recorded in a book, the Bible, and it contains the greatest love story ever told between God and His chosen people. Through unearned grace, God chooses to save His people despite their repeated rebellion against Him. The Bible is divided into two major divisions--the Old Testament (before Jesus' earthly birth) and the New Testament (the story of Jesus' life and what happened after his death). Scripture tells us that the same God that created the universe and everything within it, chose to humble Himself by leaving a perfect heaven and came down to a sinful earth in the form of a helpless, human baby named Jesus. He was raised by two human parents, and He Himself was fully human, experiencing the same daily struggles and gamut of emotions as the rest of humanity. However, unlike any other human that ever lived, He lived a perfect, sinless life while preaching the gospel in word and deed to everyone around Him before enduring a painful, agonizing, and humiliating death on a cross on behalf of you and me. Three days later, as scripture from the Old Testament accurately predicted, Jesus rose from the dead, and His resurrection put a permanent end to death. Jesus died for you and me so that we may live with him forever in heaven. His death on the cross and subsequent resurrection washed away the sins of the world, so that whoever faithfully believes in Him will live with Him for eternity. God's Word does a much better job than I ever could at succinctly describing the Gospel in the following passages:

2 Corinthians 5:21 (ESV): "For our sake he (God) made him (Jesus) to be sin who knew no sin, so that in him (Jesus) we might become the righteousness of God."

1 Corinthians 15:3-4 (ESV): "...Christ died for our sins in accordance with the Scriptures, that he was buried, that he was raised on the third day in accordance with the Scriptures..."

John 3:16 (ESV): "For God so loved the world, that he gave his only Son (Jesus), that whoever believes in him should not perish but have eternal life."

Hebrews 10:14 (ESV): "For by a single offering he has perfected for all time those who are being sanctified."

RECOMMENDED READING LIST

While the Bible should be the final authority in our lives, there is much that we can learn from those that have devoted their lives to studying scripture. Many of the men and women that comprise the group of authors I have compiled below have forgotten more about the Bible than I will ever know. Please use the following list of resources to explore more deeply many of the topics that we examined throughout our study:

- *The Treasure Principle.* Randy Alcorn
- *Precept Upon Precept Bible Studies.* Kay Arthur
- *Family Driven Faith.* Voddie Baucham
- *Family Shepherds.* Voddie Baucham
- *God and Money.* Gregory Baumer and John Cortines
- *Crazy Love.* Francis Chan
- *Just Do Something.* Kevin DeYoung
- *Crazy Busy.* Kevin DeYoung
- *Conviction to Lead.* Al Mohler
- *Living by Revealed Truth.* Tom Nettles
- *Risk is Right.* John Piper
- *This Momentary Marriage.* John Piper
- *Desiring God.* John Piper
- *Teach Them Diligently.* Lou Priolo
- *24/6: A Prescription for a Healthier, Happier Life.* Matthew Sleeth, MD
- *Improving Your Serve.* Charles Swindoll
- *Hudson Taylor's Spiritual Secret.* Howard Taylor
- *Shepherding a Child's Heart.* Tedd Tripp

Made in the USA
Lexington, KY
17 July 2017